SIX FEET UNDER

SIX FEET UNDER

THE UNOFFICIAL GUIDE

PAUL CONDON

CONTENDER
BOOKS

This book is dedicated to Mark and Audrey Condon.

First published 2002 by Contender Books
Contender Books is a division of
The Contender Entertainment Group
48 Margaret Street
London W1W 8SE

This edition published 2002
1 3 5 7 9 10 8 6 4 2

ISBN 1 84357 037 8

Printed in the UK by Butler & Tanner Ltd, Frome and London
Cover designed by Burville-Riley
Interior by seagulls

**This book is an unofficial guide and should
in no way be regarded as official merchandise.**

CONTENTS

ACKNOWLEDGEMENTS

I'd like to say a great big thank you to the following people, without whose valuable contribution this book would never have either gotten off the ground or been completed.

- ✞ Jim Sangster for help with research and excellent curries.
- ✞ Louis Niebur for kicking the whole thing off and Scott Andrews for essential supplies.
- ✞ Scott, Randy and Shaun for hospitality whilst I was in LA.
- ✞ Jo Bellingham, Joe Downie, Colin Hunter, David Massey and Lizzie Jackson for letting me play.
- ✞ Everyone else in New Media for being so supportive, particularly Ian Garrard, Neil Bastian and Tracy Kuye.
- ✞ Sue Chester, Kirsty Bridge, Naseem Hossenbux and David Jackson for their enthusiasm.
- ✞ The old gang at ECS (R.I.P) for believing in me, even when some of our directors didn't – especially Torgun, Caroline, David, Andy, Ewan and Mike.
- ✞ NUSFS – all of you: Jac, Noax, Phil, Liam and of course Peter – all of you guys know a quality TV show when you see one!
- ✞ NotPlayers – utter loons, all of you. Hooooo!

And finally to the brilliant team at Contender, particularly Michele, Rebecca, Sasha and Lee. Thanks for taking the risk on me!

INTRODUCTION

'If you mix up the letters of "funeral", you get *"real fun"* – how great is that?' ~ Billy Chenowith

It is a truth universally accepted that British television is the best in the world. From the early days of network television in the 1950s, when the viewing public switched from the cinema and wireless to the goggle box to get their entertainment, everybody knows that by and large it's been British TV that has set the benchmark for quality drama. Programmes such as *Upstairs, Downstairs, I, Claudius, Brideshead Revisited* and *Pride and Prejudice* have been rightly recognised as some of the greatest TV series ever made.

However, in the past five or six years, American TV has suddenly started producing programmes that have not only reached the benchmark of the best in British television, they've surpassed it. Where Britain led the way with politically focused shows like *House of Cards* and *Yes, Minister*, the Americans are now responsible for making 22 episodes a year of the high-rating, intelligent and sophisticated White House drama *The West Wing*. The UK manages to scrape together six episodes of *A&E*, a shallow photocopy of the still astoundingly well-made *ER*. And whereas the pinnacle of British television sitcoms in the year 2002 seems to be *My Hero* (possibly one of the most juvenile programmes ever transmitted in prime time – and that includes *It's a Royal Knockout*), the Americans give us the witty and bawdy *Sex and the City*.

And then there's *Six Feet Under*.

When a single drama series gets nominated for 23 Emmy Awards and wins the Golden Globe Award for Best Drama Series, you know it's going to be something quite special. And if that same programme was created by and continues to be produced (and occasionally written and directed) by Alan Ball of *American Beauty* fame, then you know you're looking at a product that has been created by someone with artistic vision and integrity.

One of the main reasons that *Six Feet Under* is able to break through the barriers of predictability and responsibility is because of the TV network that it's broadcast on. All of the main US networks (ABC, NBC, CBS, Fox, WB and UPN) are governed by very strict codes about what is acceptable and what is not. The level of bad language, sex, nudity and violence that can be shown on the main networks is therefore strictly controlled. Furthermore, as these networks carry advertising, they have to produce programmes within which companies are willing to purchase advertising time. Programmes that are controversial, which offend 'family values' groups that claim to represent large segments of the TV audience, are very rarely given the green light to go into production.

In 1972, a cable channel called Home Box Office (HBO) started broadcasting, initially just showing Hollywood movies. Viewers at home could pay a monthly subscription fee in order to watch the latest films, all of which were broadcast uncut – even the R-rated ones (the equivalent of the UK's 18 certificate). Eventually, HBO decided to start producing its own programmes, all of which could be free from the usual restrictions: after all, if people have been watching movies with bad language and sex in them, why shouldn't they be able to see TV programmes that deal with adult themes and storylines too? In the past few years HBO has been responsible for some of the most challenging and intelligent programming anywhere in the world, from mafia drama *The Sopranos* and gritty prison saga *Oz* through to the witty and risqué *Sex and the City*.

When Alan Ball won the Oscar for his very first movie screenplay (*American Beauty*), most pundits might have expected him to continue his career in a similar fashion. When it was announced that his next project would be a television programme based upon a dysfunctional family of funeral directors, it's safe to say that many industry pundits were somewhat surprised. Why would anyone enjoying such massive success in the film industry lower themselves to working on TV? Well, the answer to that question is obvious to anyone who has seen the series. The format of a regular weekly TV series enables the production team to tell a story that evolves over a long period of time, which can go into much more depth than a single feature film would be able to do. And that is the primary reason for *Six Feet Under* being the worldwide success that it is today.

• • •

This book is an 'unofficial' guide to *Six Feet Under*, which means that as the writer of this book I've got nothing to do with HBO, Greenblatt-Janollari Productions, Actual Size Films, Alan Ball, or any other member of the production team. I'm just a very enthusiastic fan of the programme, and I hope that if you're reading this book then you're a big fan of *Six Feet Under* too. The aim of this book is basically to highlight the best elements of the programme, to pick out the wittiest lines of dialogue, the cleverest moments of character development, and the moments that you really shouldn't be watching with your Aunt Betty from Cheadle Hulme. As a fan of the show, I'm obviously going to praise *Six Feet Under* wherever that praise is due – however, I won't hold back from mentioning those few occasions when I don't think everything hangs together quite as well as it does throughout the rest of the series.

This book will list each of the 26 episodes of *Six Feet Under* that have so far been made and broadcast in the USA. Each episode will be broken down into a number of different categories, which will enable me to examine different elements of the programme in greater detail. Not every episode will feature every category, but the general outline of the book is as follows:

EPISODE TITLE: No episodes of *Six Feet Under* have an on-screen title, but each does have its own name! These episode titles can prove to be particularly important in understanding the themes and characters of *Six Feet Under*, so it's wise to bear them in mind if you're rewatching the episodes or seeing them for the first time.

WRITER/DIRECTOR CREDITS: In any TV programme, it's the writer and director who are most responsible for the content, look and feel of the finished programme. They are detailed here so you can spot which talented individuals have contributed to your favourite episodes.

GUEST CAST: Aside from the regular cast members, this section details the actors who appear in each episode. I've divided the list into two sections – the actors who make more than one appearance in the series, and the one-off guest performers.

PLOT SUMMARY: As any good undertaker knows, choosing the right plot is very important! This section tells the story of each episode in some detail, showing how the lives of the Fisher family and their friends and relations twist and turn around each other. This section does reveal everything that happens in each episode, so if you don't want to have future storylines spoiled, don't read on!

THE PRODIGAL SON: Detailing the life, loves and character development of Nate Fisher. In particular, this section also covers Nate's relationship with the ever-unpredictable Brenda Chenowith.

ANAL CONTROL FREAK: Younger brother David Fisher is a detail-obsessed, organised control freak, a bit of an anal retentive about trying to keep his life in some kind of order. He also has a secret that he wants to keep hidden from everyone...

MOMMY, DEAREST: Ruth Fisher is a devoted and dedicated mother to her three children, but she's the kind of woman who knows what's best for them – whether they agree with her or not!

TEENAGE KICKS: As the youngest of the Fisher family, Claire has a lot to rebel against. Despite the constrictive nature of her family, Claire is a free spirit who wants to be able to express herself, and this section details her attempts to be her own young woman.

DREAM ON, DREAMER: One of the most distinctive ways in which *Six Feet Under* tells its stories is through numerous fantasy and dream sequences. This section summarises the flashbacks, song and dance routines and daydreams that the characters experience.

SOUNDTRACK: Every episode of *Six Feet Under* features a fantastic, imaginative and esoteric soundtrack that mixes classical music with contemporary urban and dance sounds. Rather than spend hours racking your brain trying to work out what each particular track is, just consult this handy guide for a quick way to locate the music that you love.

SEX, DRUGS AND ROCK 'N' ROLL: Even bearing in mind that *Six Feet Under* is shown on an American pay-TV channel, it really does push the boundaries of what can be shown in a TV drama series. In this section you'll find all the things that'll make you say: 'They can't show that on telly!' – the kind of thing that might spur 'Disgusted of Tunbridge Wells' to write to the *Daily Mail*.

THE BRIGHT SIDE OF DEATH: For a programme that is allegedly a 'drama series', *Six Feet Under* certainly makes you laugh a heck of a lot. This section pulls out the funniest and most quotable moments for your future reference.

ISN'T THAT WHATSHISNAME?: One of the most frustrating things about watching any film or TV show is when you spot somebody in the cast but you just can't place where you've seen them before. In this section you'll find a potted history of many of the cast, essentially listing the movies or TV shows that British audiences might be familiar with.

UNANSWERED QUESTIONS: The kind of things you might be left thinking about as an episode ends – or the things you might have overlooked.

EULOGY: The final summing up. In this section I will give my overall opinion of each episode and point out specific elements of interest. Like any sermon, it hopefully won't bore the congregation too much…

REGULAR CHARACTERS, CAST AND CREW

REGULAR CHARACTERS

Nate Fisher	Peter Krause
David Fisher	Michael C. Hall
Brenda Chenowith	Rachel Griffiths
Ruth Fisher	Frances Conroy
Claire Fisher	Lauren Ambrose
Federico Diaz	Freddy Rodriguez
Keith Charles	Mathew St Patrick
Billy Chenowith	Jeremy Sisto
	(Season One, Episodes 5-13)

REGULAR CAST

Peter Krause (Nate) was born on August 12, 1965 in Minnesota. He's been acting for many years and has had guest appearances in the TV series *Seinfeld, Beverly Hills, 90210, Ellen, Caroline in the City, Cybill, Party of Five* and *Third Rock From the Sun*. Peter's also had movie experience in the films *The Truman Show* and *It's a Shame About Ray*. Before becoming a professional actor, Peter used to compete in gymnastic tournaments – his specialities being the pommel horse and the rings. His partner is actress Alicia Witt and in 2001 Peter became the proud father of a son, Roman.

Michael C. Hall (David) was born on February 1, 1971 in North Carolina. Michael has made a name for himself as the star of many Broadway shows and several seasons of Shakespeare off-Broadway. One of his most famous roles has been as the MC in *Cabaret*, and over summer 2002 he guest starred in the Broadway production of *Chicago*. Michael is married to fellow Broadway actress Amy Spanger. *Six Feet Under* is Michael's first television role.

Frances Conroy (Ruth) was born on November 13, 1953 in Georgia. In 1992 Frances married actor Jan Munroe – they have one child together. Conroy's Broadway credits include *Ring Round the Moon, The Little Foxes, The Rehearsal* (Drama Desk nominee), *Broken Glass, In the Summer House* (Drama Desk nominee) and *The Secret Rapture* (Drama Desk nominee). Her numerous off-Broadway plays include *The Dinner Party, The Skin of Our Teeth, The Last Yankee* and *Othello* (Drama Desk nominee). For television, Frances has appeared in *The Royal Romance of Charles and Diana; LBJ – The Early Years* and *Alex Haley's Queen*. She has also made numerous guest appearances in TV shows as varied as *Law & Order, The Twilight Zone* and *Remington Steele*. On the big screen, Frances can be seen in *Dirty Rotten Scoundrels, Crimes and Misdemeanors, Billy Bathgate, Scent of a Woman, Sleepless in Seattle, The Crucible* and the forthcoming *Die Mommie Die* – amongst many others.

Lauren Ambrose (Claire) is still very young, being born on February 20, 1978 in Connecticut. Lauren comes from Italian parentage – her birth name was Lauren Anne D'Ambruoso. She's a classically trained opera singer and lives in Los Angeles with her husband Sam Handel. Lauren had a variety of roles in the TV series *Law & Order* before joining the cast of *Party of Five* as a regular in its sixth season. She has appeared in the films *Can't Hardly Wait* and *In & Out* (opposite Kevin Kline and Tom Selleck).

Rachel Griffiths (Brenda) was born in Queensland in 1968 and was raised in Melbourne. Yes, despite her flawless Californian accent in *Six Feet Under*, she is a true Aussie! Her breakthrough movie role came in 1994 when she played Rhonda in the world-wide smash-hit comedy *Muriel's Wedding*. Since then she's appeared in over 30 movies, including *Jude, My Best Friend's Wedding, Hilary and Jackie, Blow Dry* and *Very Annie Mary*. Her next major role will be opposite fellow Australian Heath Ledger in *The Kelly Gang*, a movie about Australia's most famous outlaw Ned Kelly. Rachel also wrote and directed the 1998 film *Tulip*, the story of a man coming to terms with his wife's death. In June 2002 she got engaged to artist Andrew Taylor.

Freddy Rodriguez (Rico) was born in 1975 and started his acting career in Lincoln Park High School, Chicago. Before *Six Feet Under*, he appeared in a variety of movies such as *Dead Presidents, The Pest, Can't Hardly Wait* and in a small role opposite Mel Gibson in *Payback*. He also appeared in the TV series *Oh Grow Up* and as a recurring character in the fifth season of *Party of Five*.

Mathew St Patrick (Keith) began his acting career with the Hudson Theater, Vincent Chase Workshop and Fine Art Dance Space, amongst others. Prior to *Six Feet Under*, he had appeared regularly in legendary daytime soap operas *General Hospital* and *All My Children*. Presumably his acting name was decided upon because he was born on March 17!

Jeremy Sisto (Billy) was born on October 6, 1974 in Northern California. He studied at UCLA for a while before becoming a full-time actor. He has appeared in more than 30 films, from *Grand Canyon* in 1991 through to *Clueless, White Squall* and *Angel Eyes*. His next TV project is playing the title role in a mini-series of the life of Julius Caesar.

REGULAR CREW

Alan Ball, the creator of *Six Feet Under*, was born in 1957 and graduated from the Florida State University School of Theater. He has worked as a writer on the TV sitcoms *Grace Under Fire* (from 1994 to 1995) and *Cybill* from 1995 to 1998, at which point he wrote the screenplay for the Academy Award-winning movie *American Beauty* (Sam Mendes, 1999). Alan has also acted as producer on many of his TV shows, including *Cybill, Oh Grow Up* and *Six Feet Under.*

Alan Poul (Executive Producer) is a veteran of both motion pictures and television. Over his fifteen-year career, he has received an Emmy Award, a Golden Globe, three Emmy nominations, three GLAAD Awards and two Peabody Awards. He was Executive Producer on *Armistead Maupin's Further Tales of the City* and *My So-Called Life* on television, and has produced many feature films including *Candyman, Black Rain* and *Mishima.*

Robert Greenblatt and **David Janollari** (Executive Producers) have forged distinguished careers as Executive Producers on many main-stream television hits, including *The Hughleys, To Have and To Hold, Maggie Winters, Oh Grow Up, The Chronicle, One On One, Definitely Maybe, American Family,* and of course *Six Feet Under.*

SEASON ONE CREW

Executive Producers:	Alan Ball, Robert Greenblatt, David Janollari
Co-Executive Producers:	Alan Poul, Christian Williams
Supervising Producer:	Bruce Eric Kaplan
Producers:	Rick Cleveland, Laurence Andries, Christian Taylor
Co-Producer:	Lori Jo Nemhauser
Co-Producer/Unit Production Manager:	Robert del Valle
Story Editor:	Kate Robin

SEASON TWO CREW

Executive Producers:	Alan Ball, Robert Greenblatt, David Janollari, Alan Poul
Co-Executive Producer:	Bruce Eric Kaplan
Supervising Producers:	Rick Cleveland, Scott Buck, Laurence Andries
Producers:	Christian Taylor, Jill Soloway
Co-Producer:	Lori Jo Nemhauser
Co-Producer/Unit Production Manager:	Robert del Valle
Executive Story Editor:	Kate Robin
Script Supervisor:	Kim Berner

SEASON ONE

EPISODE 1
SIX FEET UNDER
(PILOT EPISODE)

Directed by: Alan Ball
Written by: Alan Ball

GUEST CAST
Richard Jenkins as Nathaniel Fisher Sr
Dina Waters as Tracy Montrose Blair (Chatty Mourner)
Garrison Hershberger as Matthew Gilardi (Kroehner Representative)
Eric Balfour as Gabe Dimas (Claire's Meth Boyfriend)
Tim Maculan as Father Jack – uncredited
Jeremy Sisto as Billy Chenowith – uncredited
Hayden Tank as Young Nate
Maximillian Orion Kesmodel as Young David

Sharon Madden as Woman Mourner
Dennis Anderson as Market Clerk
Harper Roisman as Elderly Man
Dennis J. Lau as Morgue Attendant
Audrey Gelfand as Crying Sicilian Mother
Jennifer Griffin as Crying Sicilian Daughter

WHO'S THE STIFF?

Nathaniel Samuel Fisher, June 9, 1943 – December 24, 2000: It's Christmas Eve 2000, and funeral director Nathaniel Fisher is driving to collect his son Nate from the airport. Nathaniel's wife Ruth calls him and reminds him to collect some extra ingredients for their Christmas dinner. Ruth nags him because she can hear that he's smoking, telling him that cigarettes will be the death of him. Nathaniel finishes the call to his wife, and whilst he is trying to light another cigarette, fails to notice a 'stop' sign in the road. A bus smashes into the side of Nathaniel's car at full speed, wrecking the brand new hearse and snapping Nathaniel's neck.

PLOT SUMMARY

At home, Ruth is preparing food for the next day's Christmas dinner. She confides in her youngest son David that she's quite glad Nathaniel is working through his 'mid-life crisis' by buying a new car rather than by having an affair with another woman – 'or heaven forbid, a man'. David seems uncomfortable with his mother's comments, but says nothing.

At Los Angeles Airport, Nate Fisher arrives from Seattle for his Christmas gathering with his family. He's been chatting on the plane with an attractive young woman. She's a professional Shiatsu masseuse, and she offers to give him a free massage. Nate gives her his phone number and asks her to give him a call. Nate looks around for his father, who is supposed to be collecting him from the airport. The young woman offers to give Nate a ride – Nate is grateful, but tells her that his father should be along shortly. 'I wasn't talking about that kind of ride,' flirts the woman. Moments later, they are having energetic, sweaty, 'kinda disgusting' sex in a cleaners' cupboard at the airport.

Back at Fisher & Sons Funeral Home, David is attending to another client when he receives a call from his younger sister Claire. She tries to get out of coming home for the gathering, but David tells her it's important. Claire angrily agrees to come home, but tells David she has to stop off at a friend's house en route.

Ruth is putting the finishing touches to a roast dinner when she gets a call informing her about Nathaniel's accident. She goes berserk and starts to trash the kitchen, sobbing hysterically. David, downstairs in the funeral home slumber room, hears the commotion and rushes upstairs, where his mother tells him what's happened.

In the airport cupboard, Nate gets a call from David, breaking the news to him. Moments later, David calls Claire. She's at a friend's house, where the 'party' is getting extremely illegal. Just before Claire takes David's call, her friend Gabe passes her some crystal meth, which she inhales. Upon hearing the news, the drug begins to kick in, and Claire heads home. The mysterious woman from the airport drives Nate to the hospital where Nathaniel's body is. She tells Nate that she's in no great hurry to get home for her family's 'annual Christmas massacre' either – she gives Nate the impression that her family is quite dysfunctional too. Nate angrily tells the woman he can't believe that such a cautious, repressed man could have been killed in a car crash. She asks him if he's angry with his father or angry that we all have to die. Nate is taken aback and wonders if the woman is a psychiatrist – she is very quick to tell him that no, she's not, but both of her parents are.

In shock over his father's death, David is finding it increasingly difficult to maintain his professional demeanour at work – he still has to ensure that the viewing of his latest client goes smoothly. In fact, when a rather over-enthusiastic young woman (the as-yet unnamed Tracy Montrose Blair) congratulates him on his work, he suddenly realises that he is now in overall charge of Fisher & Sons, and that any plans he might have for the rest of his career are, to all intents and purposes, over. Claire is finding things difficult too. Driving her mother to the hospital to identify Nathaniel's body, Ruth asks her if she's having sex or taking drugs. Claire, who's finding it hard to hang on to her emotions because of the drugs she has taken, reassures her mother that everything is OK.

At the hospital, Nate, Ruth and Claire are reunited. The young woman introduces herself to Ruth – her name is Brenda Chenowith. Ruth tells Nate that he will have to identify Nathaniel's body – to Ruth, corpses are work, not family. Claire then confides in Nate that she is high – he tells her to pull herself together and stop freaking out. As the family head home, Brenda wishes Nate all the best in coping with this terrible situation.

David is surprised that the other family members didn't bring Nathaniel's body home, and he and Nate have an argument that makes it clear that there is not much love lost between them. David then goes back to the hospital morgue to collect his father's body so that the Fisher & Sons restoration expert, Federico 'Rico', Diaz can start his work as quickly as possible. While Rico and David work on Nathaniel, David receives a phone call – it's from his boyfriend Keith Charles. David walks out of the preparation room to take the call in private, explaining to Keith why he won't be able to spend Christmas Eve with him. Keith is very supportive and tells David that he doesn't need to go through this terrible time on his own. In the preparation room, Rico shows Nate photographs of the restorations he is particularly proud of, before showing him a photo of his son, who is now almost four years old. Nate is surprised when Rico announces that his wife Vanessa is pregnant again. At that moment, a rather curt David interrupts their conversation, reminding Rico that he needs to pay attention to the preparation of Nathaniel.

Nate goes to speak to Claire, who is extremely upset and vulnerable. They take a trip to their local supermarket to collect some last-minute items for Christmas Day. Whilst they are in the store, Nate gets a call from Brenda. She's at her home, and in the background the sounds of an argument can be heard. Brenda and Nate have an argument, and Brenda hangs up on him. Claire begins to flip out completely and Nate takes her home.

Christmas morning, and the whole family is finding it very difficult to cope. David is working to reconstruct his father's face and is haunted by Nathaniel's ghost, who taunts him that he's not good enough to do the job properly. Whilst David is talking to his father, Rico turns up to give him a hand, despite the fact that it's Christmas morning. Nate goes for a jog, during which he briefly stops and imagines what it would be like if he threw himself in front of a bus.

It's the day of Nathaniel's viewing, and Nate and Claire are having a tête-à-tête. They both look at each other's lives and think that the other one has it easy – Nate envies Claire's stable family life, Claire envies Nate's freedom. David is horrified when his boyfriend Keith shows up. Keith has just finished his shift as a member of the Los Angeles Police Department, and has come to pay his respects. It's clear that David is not 'out' as a gay man to his family, and Keith showing up could expose this fact to his family. Ruth comes over to speak to David, and is shocked to see him talking to a policeman. David lies to Ruth, telling her that he and Keith 'play racquetball together'.

Nate is very uncomfortable with the sterile nature of the grief on display in a typical Fisher & Sons funeral. He tells Claire about a group of mourning women he once saw in Sicily and the hysterical way they react. He believes such unconstrained behaviour is scary, but in the long run it's a lot healthier than this calm, neatly organised mourning. Ruth breaks down in tears, and David steers her to a quiet area away from the rest of the gathering. Ruth blurts out a terrible secret to her two sons – she had been cheating on her husband for years before his death, with a widower hairdresser. David tries to make Ruth stop telling them the gory details, whereas Nate, although horrified, thinks it's probably good for her to get this off her chest. Meanwhile, outside in the main slumber room, Claire has spotted Keith and goes over to chat to him, thinking that he's 'hot'. Keith introduces himself to Claire, and tells her that he's a friend of David's. Just then, David drags him away, desperate to tell somebody about Ruth's confession. Claire observes David and Keith being very close to each other, and puts two and two together about her brother's sexuality.

Nate comforts his mother in her hour of need, telling her that he's sure that both his father and God will forgive her for her infidelity. Whilst he is comforting her, he ignores a phone call from Brenda. She is in the kitchen of her parents' house, when a dishevelled, sobbing young man walks past and takes some olives from the refrigerator.

Nathaniel's funeral is conducted by Father Jack, the Fishers' parish priest and friend. The service goes very well until Nate rails against the neatness and sterility of the service. Instead of using the delicate soil shaker to throw earth onto his father's coffin, he picks up a handful and throws it on himself, much to David's horror. Ruth then follows Nate's example, but instead of throwing just one handful onto the coffin, puts handful after handful into the grave before falling to her knees and sobbing over her husband's body.

When the funeral service finishes, Rico drives Ruth and Claire back to the family home. Nate and David exchange yet more harsh words with each other. David is furious with Nate for undermining the job both he and his father have dedicated their lives to, and tells him as much. Not only that, but he also blames Nate for abandoning the family, for leaving him to take over. As David storms away, he is approached by a young businessman from Kroehner Services International. The man seems to be offering David the option of selling Fisher & Sons to his company, but David doesn't want to hear any of it. The man tells David he'll call him when he's recovered from his loss.

Brenda arrives at the graveyard to talk to Nate. He tells her that he's a 'fucking mess', but this doesn't seem to put Brenda off. She gives him her phone number and tells him to call her. David, an emotional mess, finally shows up at Keith's apartment. They kiss, and Keith holds David close.

Nate wakes up, having dreamt of his father when he and David were little boys. Ruth enquires if Nate has to go back to Seattle soon and he tells her it's OK for him to stay for a while. He goes for a run, and imagines that he sees his father sitting on the other side of the street, waiting for a bus. As Nate watches, Nathaniel gets on the bus and waves goodbye.

THE PRODIGAL SON

In the pilot episode of *Six Feet Under*, the character that the audience is asked to identify with is Nate Fisher, because his journey of discovery most closely matches our own. As Nate meets the mysterious Brenda, and as he tries to come to terms with his father's death, we discover things at exactly the same time that he does. As Nate begins to discover that he really doesn't know his family very well at all, we also realise that Nate isn't the happy, carefree young man that his family seem to believe he is. Yes, he has his own life in Seattle – steady job, his own apartment and lots of regular casual sex – but Nate knows there is something missing from his life. Can the family he ran away from provide him with that vital missing ingredient?

ANAL CONTROL FREAK

The polar opposite of his elder brother, David Fisher is a young man who has immersed himself in what he sees to be his duty – to continue the success of the family business, to behave in a proper, dignified fashion, and to avoid embarrassing and upsetting the Fishers by being truthful about his own sexuality. However, this unstinting dedication to his 'duty' has deeply damaged him – he has repressed feelings and behaviour patterns that would enable him to be a truly happy person. This repression appears to have spread into other areas of his life too, making David unable to show affection to his family. David's anger towards his brother Nate is particularly vociferous, and perhaps quite understandable. David feels as though he did the 'right thing' by staying at home and spending his life working for the family business while his brother effectively abandoned him. David's journey through these personal issues will take a great deal of time, and will form the emotional core to the first season of *Six Feet Under*.

MOMMY, DEAREST

Ruth Fisher is actually far more complex a character than she first appears. Initially, Ruth's 'control freak' tendencies are apparent, particularly in the conversation she has with her husband prior to his accident. Even as she is desperately trying to hold her life together as she travels to the hospital to collect Nathaniel's body, she uses that time to try to maintain control over her daughter. None of these behaviour patterns are deliberately malicious, though – Ruth is simply trying to ensure that she doesn't lose any more of her family. Her breakdown by the side of Nathaniel's grave gives us an insight into her real character: a frightened and lonely lady, who despite her affair still loved her husband very much. Ruth is scared of what the future will hold for her, and is forced to resort to her old habit of emotional manipulation so that her eldest son Nate will stay around to look after her for as long as possible. As the series progresses, Ruth will have to learn how to let go or she will drive those who love her still further away.

TEENAGE KICKS

Just like most teenagers, Claire is exploring how far she can exert her own authority in her family. Typically, on the night when she first experiments with hard drugs, she is plunged into the nightmare of her father's death. Claire's reaction to Nathaniel's demise is slightly selfish, but it needs to be acknowledged that this may be due to the effect of the crystal meth. Claire is not a bratty little teenager so commonly seen in many films and TV shows: underneath her spiky exterior, she is a genuinely nice person. When she discovers the secret about David's sexuality, she doesn't use that information for her own ends – she keeps the secret, not even letting David know that she has guessed exactly who Keith is.

DREAM ON, DREAMER

In this pilot episode, we are introduced to the dramatic device that sets *Six Feet Under* apart from every other TV show. The principal characters are often to be seen interacting with the 'ghosts' of the people who have been brought to Fisher & Sons Funeral Home for embalming, reconstruction and viewing. In all of these cases, though, these 'ghosts' only ever appear when the characters are on their own. To all intents and purposes, the 'ghosts' are projections of character traits the particular individual sees within himself or herself. As such, these discussions show the true inner feelings of characters, their hidden perspectives, and the things that they are not prepared to reveal to themselves just yet.

As the death of Nathaniel has such a massive impact on the Fisher family, it's not surprising that his ghost crops up more often than any other character. David is taunted about not being talented enough at reconstruction work to do a good job on his father's head injuries, while Nate gets a stern reminder that he has tried to escape death for too long. Ruth is told that he knows about her affair. Finally, Claire sees her father, but has a very pleasant chat with him whilst sharing a cigarette.

There are many other instances of fantasy/dream sequences in this pilot episode. David imagines losing control and screaming his pain out loud in the middle of a viewing, shortly before the chatty Tracy Montrose Blair corners him. He imagines her making offensive comments before he actually does scream out loud in front of the group of mourners. When Nate goes back down to the preparation room for the first time since coming home, he gets a flashback to a time when he was a child and his father invited him to touch a body he was working on. Trying to come to terms with his loss, Nate goes for a jog and momentarily imagines what would happen if he ended it all by throwing himself in front of a bus. In this fantasy, blood leaks from a wound in his head (the location of the wound will become significant in the second series) and he then goes to heaven and imagines seeing his father, naked, playing poker with a group of similarly nude corpses. Nate's final dream is of seeing his father getting on board the bus that killed him and waving goodbye – an image that will continue to haunt him throughout the rest of *Six Feet Under*.

SOUNDTRACK

Bizet – 'L'amour Est Un Oiseau Rebelle' (First commercial break for the upmarket Hearse)

Bing Crosby – 'I'll Be Home For Christmas' (Nathaniel's crash)

Hardknox – 'Attitude' (Claire phones David from her car)

Spylab – 'Celluloid Hypnotic' (Claire smokes crystal meth and finds out her dad is dead)

Tommaso Giovanni Albinoni – 'Concerto For Oboe & String In D. Major, Allegro E Non-Presto' (David tries to hold his emotions in check at the funeral viewing)

Petalpusher – 'Breaking It Down' ('Living Splendor' embalming fluid)

Peggy Lee – 'I Love Being Here With You' (Flashback to Nathaniel speaking to his boys)

Les Gammas – 'All Of Me' (David gets a call from Keith)

Ray Davies – 'Sunset Seranade' (Wound-filler commercial break)

Day One – 'Bedroom Dancing' (Nate's dream of a bus crash)

The Executives – 'Moonglow Cha Cha Cha' (Nate's morgue poker dream)

Wolfgang Amadeus Mozart – 'Divertimento #1, Andante' (Nathaniel's wake)
KC and the Sunshine Band – 'Shake Your Booty' (Commercial break for soil shakers)
The Devlins – 'Waiting' (Nate sees Nathaniel wave goodbye on the bus)

SEX, DRUGS AND ROCK 'N' ROLL

Not a huge amount on display in this first episode, but what there is is quite shocking. Nate and Brenda enjoy their infamous airport cupboard encounter at roughly the same time that Claire is smoking crystal meth for the first time.

THE BRIGHT SIDE OF DEATH

Brenda: How's it going with you?
Nate: Great. My father's dead, my mom's a whore, my brother wants to kill me and my sister's smoking crack. I think I win.

Nate: The only father we're ever going to have is gone. For ever. And that sucks... I intend to honour the old bastard by letting the whole world see just how fucked up and shitty I feel that he's dead! (He throws the fistful of earth onto the coffin.) Goddammit!
Father Jack: Erm... Amen.

Nate: I also happen to be a serial rapist. I've got ten nurses buried under my house.
Brenda: Now you're making me wet...

ISN'T THAT WHATSHISNAME?

Richard Jenkins (Nathaniel Fisher Sr) played Kelly the Gambler in *Silverado* (Lawrence Kasdan, 1985), Dr Wilkes in *Hannah and her*

Sisters (Woody Allen, 1986), Clyde Alden in *The Witches of Eastwick* (George Miller, 1987), Gruber in *Sea of Love* (Harold Becker, 1989), Attorney Mel Dawson in *Blue Steel* (Kathryn Bigelow, 1990), Truman Trainor in *Random Hearts* (Sidney Pollack, 1999), Agent Boshane in *Me, Myself and Irene* (Bobby & Peter Farrelly, 2000) and Walter Abundas in *The Man Who Wasn't There* (Joel Coen, 2001). **Dina Waters** (Tracy Montrose Blair) – née Dina Spybey – can be seen in the films *The First Wives Club* (Hugh Wilson, 1996), *Striptease* (Andrew Bergman, 1996), *SubUrbia* (Richard Linklater, 1996) and *An Alan Smithee Film: Burn Hollywood Burn* (Arthur Hiller – as Alan Smithee – 1997) as well as playing Brenda Mikowski in the American version of the sitcom *Men Behaving Badly*. **Garrison Hershberger** (Matthew Gilardi) – often credited as Gary Hershberger – played Mike Nelson in the surreal TV drama *Twin Peaks*, amongst many bit parts in film and TV.

Sharon Madden (Woman Mourner) appeared in *Jagged Edge* (Richard Marquand, 1985), *Two Moon Junction* (Zalman King, 1988) and *Turner & Hooch* (Roger Spottiswoode, 1989). Despite being just eleven years old, **Hayden Tank** (Young Nate) has already amassed some impressive credits: he played Eric Braeden's son in the soap opera *The Young and the Restless* from 1997-99, a young Brendan Fraser in *Blast from the Past* (Hugh Wilson, 1999), Ben Kingsley's son in *Rules of Engagement* (William Friedkin, 2000), John C. Reilly's son in *The Perfect Storm* (Wolfgang Petersen, 2000) and had a small part in *Space Cowboys* (Clint Eastwood, 2000). **Dennis Anderson** (Market Clerk) played the manager of Mr Smiley's Burgers in Alan Ball's big-screen success *American Beauty* (Sam Mendes, 1999). **Audrey Gelfand** (Crying Sicilian Mother) appeared in *Being John Malkovich* (Spike Jonze, 1999), while **Jennifer Griffin** (Crying Sicilian Daughter) had small roles in *A Perfect World* (Clint Eastwood, 1993) and *Vanilla Sky* (Cameron Crowe, 2001)

UNANSWERED QUESTIONS

✟ Will this family ever be able to sort through their problems?
✟ Will David be able to come out to his family?

✝ Will Nate stay in Los Angeles?
✝ Will Ruth continue her relationship with her hairdresser?
✝ Will Claire continue to do drugs?
✝ Will the ghost of Nathaniel continue to haunt the family?
✝ Who was the man who offered to buy out Fisher & Sons?
✝ Who was the crying man in Brenda's house?

EULOGY

A simply stunning start to the series, the pilot episode for *Six Feet Under* is almost unique amongst modern television series in so far as it tells a complete story and doesn't rely upon cheap cliffhanger endings or over-the-top histrionics to get viewers to tune in again the following week. In this respect, this first episode is very filmic – surely a consequence of Alan Ball's close involvement in the programme. It's almost as though we have seen everything that we need to see. If *Six Feet Under* had never progressed beyond a one-off episode, we would not feel too cheated, as the plotting and structure of this hour feel so 'complete' and 'finished'. Thankfully, however, there is a great deal more to the story of the Fishers still to be told! One element from this first episode which is sadly missing from subsequent episodes is the mock adverts for funeral products, a hilarious indictment of the way in which consumerism can market almost anything and make it seem palatable. A fantastic start to *Six Feet Under*, which gets better with each subsequent viewing.

EPISODE 2
THE WILL

Directed by: Miguel Arteta
Written by: Christian Williams

GUEST CAST
Ed Begley Jr as Hiram
Garrison Hershberger as Matthew Gilardi
Justina Machado as Vanessa Diaz
Eric Balfour as Gabe Dimas
Maximillian Orion Kesmodel as Young David

Tracy Middendorf as Adele Swanson
Missy Yager as Jennifer Mason
Mark Devine as Chandler Swanson
Daniel Zacapa as Mr Suarez Jr
Richard Penn as Attorney
Melissa Egan as Debbie
Chip O'Neil as Ronnie
Van Epperson as Angry Man

WHO'S THE STIFF?

Chandler James Swanson, 1967-2001: The dynamic, go-getting inventor of an infomercial franchise called 'Beauty Vision' discovered that diving head first into a swimming pool can have less than beautiful consequences. He smashed his head on the bottom of the pool, leaving a distraught wife and young baby.

PLOT SUMMARY

January 8, 2001. David wakes up with a jolt in Keith's apartment. He tells his boyfriend that he has to rush – today is the day of the reading of his father's will. As David leaves, Keith reminds him that they are both due to attend his Gay Police and Firemen's Club the following night.

David and Nate (who has spent the night at Brenda's) arrive home at Fisher & Sons at the same time. Nate notices that David's wearing the same clothes as last night and teases him about it, but Claire – who has realised that her brother is gay and incredibly uncomfortable about admitting the fact – tells Nate to leave David alone. David has an intake meeting with young widow Adele Swanson. When she reveals that her late husband was a wealthy BMW-driving entrepreneur, David encourages Adele to choose the most expensive coffin in their range, the Titan, as it is a 'statement' about the kind of man he was.

The whole Fisher clan then assembles at their lawyer's office for the reading of Nathaniel's will. Ruth is left a cool $500,000 in life insurance. Claire is upset that 'all' she gets in the will is the money to pay for her college education, with an added stipulation that if the money isn't used for that purpose, she is unable to have it until her 25th birthday. Claire feels as though her father is blackmailing her from beyond the grave into conforming. However, the real trouble comes when the fate of the business is revealed. Instead of, as expected, leaving Fisher & Sons for David to manage on his own, Nathaniel splits the company evenly between his two sons. David is deeply upset at this perceived betrayal and storms out of the lawyer's office. For his part, Nate is equally angry at his father – he wants nothing to do with the family business, and resents the fact that he's been forced by Nathaniel into taking that responsibility.

Returning to the family home, David faces a problem: Rico is busy and therefore cannot collect the body of their latest client, Mr Suarez. David somewhat smugly gives Nate the job of collecting the corpse, telling his brother that it's his responsibility now he's half-owner of the company. Sensing Nate's discomfort, Rico tells him that he really isn't that busy after all – and that he'll go with him to the nursing home to collect the body.

At school, Gabe Dimas tries to chat Claire up. He tells Claire that he wants to go out with her, and while she's flattered, she isn't sure if he's just trying it on. Meanwhile, Ruth gets a caller to the house – Matthew Gilardi, the representative from Kroehner Services. He repeats the offer he made to David at Nathaniel's funeral, that his company is interested in buying out Fisher & Sons. Ruth doesn't want to hear such suggestions, and asks Gilardi to leave.

Arriving at the nursing home, Rico reintroduces Nate to his wife Vanessa, who works there as a nurse. Vanessa has some mildly inconvenient news for Rico – he's going to have to collect their son Julio from pre-school (nursery). Nate therefore has to take Mr Suarez's body back to Fisher & Sons on his own. The journey is an uncomfortable reminder of how much he hates being around the dead – he has to deal with the body's post-mortem erection ('angel lust', explains Rico), then a succession of disgusting noises as Mr Suarez's body voids its bowels.

On the way home, Nate gets a call from Brenda, who invites him to stop off and have a 'first date' with her. Nate is delighted to get away from Mr Suarez for a while and agrees. Over a few drinks, Nate tells Brenda how much he hates the funeral business, and then tells her that the idea of having a 'first date' with her is impossible – normally he just piles on the charm with women in order to have sex with them, but with her he wants something more. Brenda, for her part, tells Nate that he's far more interesting than most of the men she's met – none of them have dead guys with hard-ons in the back of their cars!

Back at home, David tells Ruth that they have a problem with Chandler Swanson's funeral – it seems that unknown to his wife, he was actually in debt over his head, and as a result, they have no money to pay for the funeral and the expensive coffin. When Nate returns with Mr Suarez's body, David berates him for leaving the corpse to decompose whilst he was off enjoying himself. That evening, Claire meets up with Gabe for a date. They sit in her car, smoking dope and chatting about each other's lives, getting along very well.

The next morning, Ruth tells her sons that she is going to go on a hike with her hairdresser, Hiram – the man she was having an affair with. David is shocked and upset, but Nate tells her to go and enjoy herself. Still feeling spiteful towards his brother, David orders Nate to break the news to Adele Swanson that she has no money to pay for the funeral she's ordered. Nate handles the situation quite well, but makes one major error when suggesting a compromise for Adele. He tells her that he will arrange for her husband to be cremated, but in order to help maintain her husband's dignity, she can have Chandler's viewing in the expensive Titan coffin. When David returns home and sees Chandler laid out in the Titan, he is almost apoplectic with rage – it's against the law to ever re-use a coffin, even if it's only been used for a few minutes. The cost of the coffin will now have to come out of the Fisher & Sons finances.

Whilst on their hike, Ruth surprises Hiram by breaking off their relationship – she's just too guilt-ridden about Nathaniel's death to carry on any longer. Back at Fisher & Sons, David gets a surprise visitor – his ex-fiancée Jennifer Mason arrives to see him, having only just heard the news about Nathaniel's death. David and Jennifer decide to go out for dinner, David having forgotten his previous arrangement to go out with Keith to the Gay Police and Firemen's Club. That same night, Claire's relationship with Gabe moves to the next level – they have sex in the back of her car, then, after he begs her, she somewhat reluctantly sucks his toes.

Keith is looking for David, and comes round to the house. He runs into Nate (who is clearing up Mr Suarez's little accident from the back of the hearse), who tells Keith that David has gone for dinner with his ex-fiancée. David's meal with Jennifer goes from bad to worse. Although Jennifer knows that David is gay (the reason they split up), David gets very drunk and ends up asking her to fuck him. She's disgusted at his behaviour and leaves. The still very merry David goes back to Keith's apartment. Keith asks where he was, and how he could have forgotten their arrangement for that night. David lies to him, saying that he had to pick up a body. Knowing full well that this is a lie, Keith shuts the door in David's face.

At Brenda's house, Nate begins to undress his new enigmatic girlfriend when something makes him stop suddenly: he's spotted a tattoo on the small of her back – the name 'Nathaniel'. Nate is freaked out, but Brenda explains that 'Nathaniel' doesn't refer to him, it's the name of somebody else who she would have done anything for, someone in her past. With Nate reassured, the two of them spend the night together.

The following morning, Nate tells Brenda that he has to go with David that afternoon to inspect the wrecked hearse in which his father died. As he leaves, Brenda tells him to take his mobile phone with him. Back at Fisher & Sons, Nate makes a deal (against David's better judgement) with Mr Suarez's son to buy the used Titan coffin at a discount. A short while later, whilst out jogging, Nate is approached by Matthew Gilardi with the offer to buy Fisher & Sons. It's clear that Nate is quite taken by the possibility of being able to offload the business.

That afternoon, David and Nate go to the garage to inspect the wrecked hearse. They need to retrieve the insurance papers from the vehicle in order to make a claim. Although Nate is deeply affected by seeing the place where his father died and the blood-stained steering wheel, David climbs calmly into the vehicle and retrieves the necessary documents. At that moment, Brenda calls Nate on his mobile, and tells him to bring David and meet her nearby. When they get to the rendezvous point, the brothers are somewhat bemused at this choice of location, until a bus pulls up and the doors open. Brenda is on board the bus and she tells the Fisher brothers to get on. They soon realise that this is *the* bus – the bus that killed their father. Nate is initially shocked and furious with Brenda, until David finally breaks down. Nate holds his brother's hand, as David sobs with grief for his dead father. Brenda smiles affectionately, having done something that has really helped her new boyfriend's family.

THE PRODIGAL SON

The more we see of the Fisher family in these first few episodes, the more we can empathise with Nate's desire to escape from their dysfunctional clutches. Naturally, this being a drama series, as soon as it looks as though Nate may be able to leave and get on with his own life again, something happens to drag him back into the family's over-protective stranglehold. By inheriting half of Fisher & Sons, Nate is forced to come to a very important, life-changing decision. Should he go back to his carefree, responsibility-lite life in Seattle, or should he do what his father and family have longed for all along – take an active role in their lives? Faced with the horror of dealing with corpses – something that has traumatised him since his childhood – it's quite surprising that Nate doesn't just grab his suitcase and leave. It seems that he is still looking for a way out that won't annoy his family too much... and that way out might just be around the corner. Underpinning all of this is his burgeoning relationship with Brenda. Following their initial lust-powered coupling in the airport cupboard, Nate seems to be just as surprised as Brenda that things are developing into something much more serious. He doesn't understand her, of course (the shock of seeing his name tattooed just above her arse almost ruins things completely), but it's that very lack of understanding that drives them further together.

ANAL CONTROL FREAK

David spends most of 'The Will' in a foul mood, a mood directed firstly at his late father, then at his interloping brother, then finally at himself for his stupid behaviour. He cannot come to terms with the fact that all the years of hard work and sacrifice he put into the family business haven't been rewarded in the way he expected. Instead of rationalising the decision (that Nathaniel had called the business 'Fisher & Sons', not 'Fisher & Son' or 'Fisher & Children'), David instead imagines the real reason he has been 'slighted' by his father. To David's mind, the only possible explanation is that he's gay, and that his father either knew or suspected the fact. With Nathaniel wanting the business to continue in the family, the only possible solution to this issue is to give half of the company to the only son who could continue the family line. There's no evidence whatsoever that Nathaniel really felt like this – it's just another of David's grandiose moments of self-loathing. David consequently spends most of the episode lashing out at Nate in a blatant case of transfer-ence. When David's ex-fiancée Jennifer turns up, he desperately attempts to create a pretence of family life, but the wise woman she is, she turns him down quickly. Turning yet another failure into an excuse for yet more self-harm, David gets drunk and screws up his real relationship with Keith by lying to him. Indeed, it's only at the very end of the episode, whilst riding the bus that killed his father, that David is finally able to let out all of these pent-up emotions – the first step on the road to dealing with the pain of bereavement.

MOMMY, DEAREST

Still reeling from the death of her husband, Ruth continues to dwell in a world of pain, guilt and recrimination. She pushes away her long-term 'bit on the side' Hiram because she can no longer deal with the knowledge that not only did she cheat on Nathaniel, but that, as he's now in heaven, he knows what went on. She snaps at Claire yet again, seemingly almost wishing for her daughter to develop an eating disorder. Ruth is still not anywhere near healthy enough to really come to terms with her bereavement – this process still has a long way to go.

TEENAGE KICKS

Claire behaves in expected fashion and manages to begin dealing with her father's death before the rest of the Fishers. She reacts angrily to the perceived blackmail of being made to remain in formal education, and finds it difficult to be persuaded that this is a display of kindness. Claire then moves on with her life, and begins a physical relationship with Gabe Dimas. Despite Claire's sarcastic exterior, all she really wants is to be loved. If her family isn't able to provide that love for her, she will seek it out somewhere else.

DREAM ON, DREAMER

David imagines seeing the ghost of his father on many separate occasions – firstly, when he's in bed with boyfriend Keith (causing him much embarrassment and shame), then criticising him for being unable to provide an heir to inherit the family business.

Nate remembers his father asking him if he wanted to touch a dead body and it proving to be far too much for the young boy to cope with. David, on the other hand, remembers the incident too, and recalls how easy it was for him to touch the corpse.

Nate's dreams reveal more about his own psyche, too. Nate dreams of his brother lying in a coffin, hurling abuse at him – 'You fucking moron!' Nate has always known that he isn't the brightest of the Fisher children, and this vision reveals his own inner insecurity. Later, Nate sees his father's ghost, belittling the text the family chose for his gravestone, then mocking the loathsome Gilardi.

Finally, David gets to see the reverse of a vision that Nate had in the first episode – whilst riding the bus, he sees his father outside on the pavement, holding him as a child, waving him goodbye.

SOUNDTRACK

Dean Martin – 'Ain't That A Kick In The Head' (Chandler Swanson's accident)
Soulstice – 'Tenderly' (David wakes up in Keith's apartment)
Submarine – 'Girl Who Fell To Earth' (Claire and Gabe talk together)
Peggy Lee – 'I Love Being Here With You' (Nate's flashback of Nathaniel offering him gloves)
The Blasters – 'So Long Baby, Goodbye' (Chandler's viewing)
The Starseeds – 'Parallel Life' (Nate discovers Brenda's tattoo)
Dandy Warhols – 'Bohemian Like You' (Nate goes jogging)

SEX, DRUGS AND ROCK 'N' ROLL

David dreams of a raunchy naked wake-up from his partner Keith (before he wakes up to a much less romantic early morning conversation!) Later on, when drunk, he asks his ex-girlfriend for sex, but thankfully for his own mental health, gets turned down by her. Claire goes all the way with Gabe, before being asked to go even further and give him a toe-job, which she reluctantly agrees to.

Must be all the dope they smoked... Brenda and Nate continue their relationship too, with Nate having stayed over at her house before the episode begins.

THE BRIGHT SIDE OF DEATH

Brenda: I don't meet that many men with dead guys with hard-ons in their car.

David: You stopped to eat? Do you have any respect for human life at all?
Nate: I have a huge respect for human life. I just didn't know they can take a dump when they're dead!

ISN'T THAT WHATSHISNAME?

Look out for **Justina Machado** (Vanessa Diaz) in Steven Spielberg's *A.I.* (2001) in which she plays an assistant. **Tracy Middendorf** (Adele Swanson)'s TV credits include daytime soap *Days of Our Lives* (as Carrie Brady) and *Beverly Hills, 90210* (as Laura Kingman). She was also in the films *Wes Craven's New Nightmare* (Wes Craven, 1994) and *For Love of the Game* (Sam Raimi, 1999). **Missy Yager** (Jennifer Mason) appears in *Dead Man Walking* (Tim Robbins, 1995). **Daniel Zacapa** (Mr Suarez Jr) can be seen in *Se7en* (David Fincher, 1995), *Up Close and Personal* (Jon Avnet, 1996), *Phenomenon* (Jon Turteltaub, 1996) and *The Mexican* (Gore Verbinski, 2001). He's also seen as a Feng Shui expert in a series of British TV adverts for Australian lager where he ends up removing the entire contents of his client's glamorous LA apartment.

UNANSWERED QUESTIONS

✝ Now that Nate owns half of Fisher & Sons, and now that his casual fling with Brenda is becoming more serious, will he decide to stay in LA or go back to his life of freedom in Seattle?

✞ Will any member of the family take up Gilardi's buy-out offer?
✞ Is Brenda telling the truth about her 'Nathaniel' tattoo? If so, exactly who did she have the tattoo done for?
✞ Will Keith be able to forgive David for lying to him?

EULOGY

Quite an unusual episode for *Six Feet Under*, this one, as it actually contains rather more plot development than character-based dialogue. Things change radically in 'The Will', not least because of the titular document. Nathaniel could probably never have predicted just how much trouble his last will and testament would cause, but we as viewers are delighted he did it that way. The family squabbles following the reading of the will are the communication low point of the whole series – everyone is angry, upset and unwilling to listen to what the other family members say or want. Indeed, it's only the behaviour of outsiders Brenda, Keith and Gabe that stops the Fisher family from imploding at this point.

EPISODE 3
THE FOOT

Directed by: John Patterson
Written by: Bruce Eric Kaplan

GUEST CAST
Garrison Hershberger as Matthew Gilardi
Eric Balfour as Gabe Dimas
Hayden Tank as Young Nate

Caroline Aaron as Amelia
John Capodice as Tommy Romano
Sandra Purpuro as Barbara Romano
Carol Ann Susi as Pauline Romano
Christina Carlisi as Judy Romano
Joe Basile as Morgue Attendant
Lindsey Parks as Jeannie Fritzen
Marty Belafsley as Bakery Worker
Christopher Michael as Deadwagon Attendant
Darren Le Gallo as School Boy #1
Scott Torrence as School Boy #2
Eric Keith as Newlywed Man
Lenora May as Freckles' Mom
Beans as Freckles

WHO'S THE STIFF?

Thomas Alfredo Romano, 1944-2001: He was cleaning out an industrial dough mixer when one of his colleagues accidentally switched the machine on, kneading and chopping him into lots of little pieces. Messy.

PLOT SUMMARY

A post-coital Nate and Brenda lie on the floor together, discussing their relationship. Nate asks her to move to Seattle to be with him, but Brenda points out that they've only just met and that such a rapid commitment would be crazy. Accepting her perspective, Nate tells her that he has to leave – there's a meeting with Matt Gilardi from Kroehner that day, where the possibility of selling Fisher & Sons to the giant corporation will be discussed. Nate tells Brenda he's hoping that his family decides to sell.

Claire is enjoying a 'morning after the night before' moment too as she comes down for breakfast. Her energetic night with Gabe has left her ravenous. As the family discuss the imminent meeting with Kroehner, Nate voices his opinion that they should sell. When Ruth agrees with Nate, David spits back at them, 'Fine. Sell. What do I care? Let's just invalidate my entire life…'

Shortly after, David has an intake meeting with Thomas Romano's widow and daughters. Despite the horrific nature of his demise, the Romanos are determined to have an open casket viewing. As Rico is busy going to the christening of his cousin's baby, David is reluctantly forced to send Nate to collect Mr Romano's remains. Mr Romano is a 'humpty dumpty' case – his body is in literally dozens of pieces. Nate struggles with the body bag, full of loose and unconnected items, dropping the bag and hitting it against walls as he gets it into the hearse.

Arriving at school, Claire is perturbed when she hears people giggling at her. When she gets back to her car, it is covered with graffiti – 'toe slut' and 'little piggy lover'. Claire finds Gabe and tears a strip off him, furious that he bragged about his conquest to his friends. He's not particularly apologetic to her, so she dumps him.

Keith and David are shopping for a ceiling fan for Keith's apartment. David is mulling over the idea of selling the business to Kroehner. By selling, he would finally be free and able to afford to do what he's always wanted to – go to law school. David is increasingly tempted by the prospect of freedom. Meanwhile, Nate is in Gilardi's office, sealing the deal to sell Fisher & Sons. Gilardi is delighted and tells Nate that he's made the right decision. However, Nate sees a vision of his father, who calls Gilardi a 'greedy little Nazi fuck'. As Nate drives home, he realises that selling the business to Kroehner makes logical and financial sense, but it means abandoning needy people to the humanity-free sausage factory that is Kroehner. Nathaniel appears to Nate once more, reminding him that he has a gift of helping people through tough times in their lives – returning to his menial job in Seattle would be throwing that gift away.

At home, Ruth is 'enjoying' a visit from one of her friends, Amelia. Amelia believes that it's her duty to force Ruth into the grieving process as quickly as possible. Ruth isn't in the mood to be forced into doing anything that will help her heal, so she rejects Amelia's advice.

That evening, Nate tells Ruth and David that he thinks they have made a bad decision – they should return Gilardi's cheque to him. David is more annoyed than ever at his brother, accusing him of being unable to make a decision and stick to it. Nate retorts by saying that he's sure this is what he's supposed to do – by working at Fisher & Sons, he can finally find a role for himself in life, and he can also get to know his family once again. Later, Nate celebrates his decision with Brenda, who is delighted that he's going to be staying in LA.

The next morning, whilst doing his best to learn the business, Nate accidentally drops the body bag containing the parts of Mr Romano. At that moment, Claire arrives to talk to Nate, but seeing him retching at the sight of the diced Mr Romano, she makes a rapid exit. David then assigns Nate a job better suited to his talents – pruning the bushes in the garden. Whilst he's hard at work, Nate is approached by Matt Gilardi, who takes a great deal of smug satisfaction in telling him that Kroehner has just bought the house on the other side of the street. They intend to develop the house into a 'Poseidon Society' – a low-cost, high-volume cremation facility. As Nate breaks the bad news to David, Rico bursts in with some bad news of his own – Mr Romano is missing a foot!

A desperate search for Mr Romano's missing foot begins, but they have no idea where it could be. The foot has in fact been stolen by Claire. When Gabe Dimas opens his locker at school that morning, he gets a rather disturbing surprise, courtesy of the vengeful toe-sucker, Ms Fisher. He screams in horror at the discovery.

Ruth, in a moment of uncharacteristic spontaneity, decides to drag her friend Amelia to the local racetrack. Although she starts off in a glum mood, she soon begins to win big money, and for the first time since Nathaniel's death, seems to be enjoying herself. David has gone to see Keith. Whilst he's there, he gets a call on his mobile from Rico, who tells him that Claire's school has been on the phone – there's been a report linking Claire to a severed foot. David panics about the news – not only could Fisher & Sons be sued for losing a part of one of their clients, but they could face criminal charges too. Keith offers to help get to the bottom of the problem – after all, he is a policeman. Keith and David go to Claire's school and question Gabe about the foot. He tells them that he was driving to show the foot to his friends when he suddenly panicked, realising he could get into trouble for being in possession of a human body part, and threw it out of his car window into a grassy field.

Meanwhile, Nate shows Brenda around the abandoned house across the street from Fisher & Sons that Kroehner has just bought. He used to play there when he was a child with his neighbour Jeannie Fritzen. Nate and Brenda make love in the house before falling asleep there. They are awoken by a call on Brenda's mobile. There's an angry man shouting and screaming on the other end of the line. Without explaining who it is, Brenda tells Nate she has to leave, but that she will call him soon and she's glad he's staying in LA.

At home that night, Ruth confesses to Nate and David that she lost more than $20,000 betting at the racetrack. The boys are, to put it mildly, shocked. At the same time, Keith bumps into Claire – they're both searching for the lost foot by cover of darkness. Claire tells Keith that she knows he's seeing David. They have a charming heart-to-heart, but sadly they fail to find the missing foot.

The following day's viewing for Mr Romano still goes well, thanks to the skills of Rico. He uses a frozen leg of lamb tucked into the bottom of the corpse's trousers to stand in for the missing foot. The deception is almost uncovered when the bereaved Mrs Romano turns into a 'casket climber' – someone so grief-stricken that they try to climb into the coffin with their dearly departed. Thankfully Mrs Romano is pulled back before she can dislodge the leg. Rico then confesses to the Fisher brothers that he lied about going to the christening – he was actually having a meeting with Gilardi, who was hoping to persuade him to join Kroehner. Rico tells David and Nate that he will be staying with Fisher & Sons.

After the service, the boys let Ruth in on what's happened with the foot. She's utterly horrified. At that precise moment, Claire walks in and casually comments that the house on the other side of the road is on fire. 'I guess this should solve all your problems, huh?' Nate looks at his sister, highly suspicious that she may have started the fire. The next morning, a woman walking her dog Freckles in a grassy field is horrified when her pooch comes trotting back with a human foot in its mouth...

THE PRODIGAL SON

Nate's reassessment of what is and isn't important in his life forms the core of this episode. He begins by asking his new girlfriend to join him in his old life in Seattle. When Brenda points out that this idea is blatantly silly, Nate tries to come up with an alternative plan, and for the first time begins to believe that working at Fisher & Sons might be a viable option for him.

ANAL CONTROL FREAK

For a short while in 'The Foot', David allows himself to think of what his life might actually be like without Fisher & Sons – and it's quite a tempting proposition. On the one hand, this is an ideal chance to start his life over again from scratch. On the other, selling out to Kroehner would effectively invalidate all of the life choices he has made so far. David is still in deep mistrust mode of his brother, so Nate's change of mind isn't the relief and validation for David that it should be – instead it's the theft of his opportunity for freedom.

MOMMY, DEAREST

One of the nicest aspects of 'The Foot' is our first chance to see Ruth actually enjoying herself. Admittedly, it does cost her over $20,000 to manage this emotional turnaround! It is the overbearing efforts of her 'friend' Amelia that helps Ruth realise how unhappy she must have been, and although there's still a long way to go before Ruth is able to really forge a new life for herself, this is the point where that journey to freedom and happiness begins.

TEENAGE KICKS

Poor Claire goes through quite an emotional rollercoaster in this episode. She starts off with her joyous song and dance routine before being rapidly brought back down to earth by the casual stupidity of Gabe and the cruelty of her classmates. Claire, though, is not the kind of girl to be kept down for long, and she grabs a spur-of-the-moment opportunity to take her revenge on Gabe. She soon realises that this moment of stupidity will have long-lasting consequences and tries to sort the problem out before her part in it is discovered. Essentially, Claire is deeply in love with Gabe. She allowed him to persuade her into taking drugs, into having sex, into giving him a toe-job. Although she feels hurt and betrayed, her love for him is not yet over and done with.

DREAM ON, DREAMER

Claire's 'What A Little Moonlight Can Do' song is a lovely, positive and upbeat moment – in stark contrast to the self-flagellating visions that Nate suffers from in this episode. First he sees his father again, berating him for selling out to Gilardi, then he even sees critical messages for him on placards being held by a group of protesters. Finally he has flashbacks of him as a boy playing with neighbour Jeannie Fritzen, before Jeannie suddenly begins to speak with Brenda's adult voice.

SOUNDTRACK

Peggy Lee – 'Things Are Swinging' (Nate and Brenda fool around)
Lauren Ambrose – 'What A Little Moonlight Can Do' (Claire's fantasy song and dance routine)
Aterciopelados – 'El Album' (Nate and Brenda celebrate Nate staying in LA)
Zero 7 – 'Distractions' (Nate and Brenda have a joint and talk)
Julie London – 'Yummy Yummy Yummy' (Little Brenda plays)

SEX, DRUGS AND ROCK 'N' ROLL

Nate and Brenda enjoy yet more private and public sex, at her flat and in the abandoned house.

THE BRIGHT SIDE OF DEATH

Nate: I'm a little busy right now, swimming in a man's guts. (Picks up a body part) I'm picking up a part of a person, and I don't even know what part it is!

Ruth: She stole a foot? From a person?
David: Yes. Would it have been better if it was an animal's?
Nate: A little bit.

Ruth: You wake up one day, and your baby's stolen a foot. Where have I been?
David: Losing $25,000.

ISN'T THAT WHATSHISNAME?

Eric Balfour (Gabriel) might be familiar to fans of *Buffy the Vampire Slayer* – he played Xander's best friend Jesse in the first two episodes of the series. He also played the boyfriend of Mel Gibson's on-screen daughter in the romantic comedy *What Women Want* (Nancy Meyers, 2000) and is a regular on one of the most talked-about shows of the year, *24*. **John Capodice** (Tommy Romano)'s film credits include *Wall Street* (Oliver Stone, 1987), *See No Evil, Hear No Evil* (Arthur Hiller, 1989), *Gremlins 2: The New Batch* (Joe Dante, 1990), *Point of No Return* (John Badham, 1993), *Speed* (Jan de Bont, 1994), *Independence Day* (Roland Emmerich, 1996) and *Enemy of the State* (Tony Scott, 1998). What a busy guy! **Sandra Purpuro** (Barbara Romano) plays Catherine McClain in another HBO drama series, the compelling prison saga *Oz*, while **Carol Ann Susi** (Pauline Romano) had a guest role in *Married... with Children*. **Christopher Michael** (Deadwagon Attendant) played Commander Rankin in the TV show *The District* (2000) and a Dam cop in the romantic comedy *Fools Rush In* (Andy Tennant, 1997).

UNANSWERED QUESTIONS

✟ Can Fisher & Sons survive the pressure that Kroehner is piling on them?
✟ Brenda joked about having used heroin in the past – is she just joking?
✟ Why did Rico turn down Gilardi's offer?
✟ Who was the angry, screaming man on the end of the phone to Brenda?
✟ Who burned down the empty house?

EULOGY

'The Foot' is really the episode that sets the benchmark for the rest of the first season of *Six Feet Under*, providing a truly ghastly death that mixes extreme body horror with guffaws of black comedy. It's the juxtaposition between the suffering and grief of the family and the comedy of searching for a severed foot that forms the thematic core for subsequent episodes – looking death square in the face and being able to laugh at it. This episode is also the point where the core characters begin to settle into their respective roles – Ruth trying to find some way forward in life, Nate finally having to take responsibility for his own life, and Claire beginning to rebuild her life with a new relationship.

EPISODE 4
FAMILIA

Directed by: Lisa Cholodenko
Written by: Laurence Andries

GUEST CAST
Garrison Hershberger as Matthew Gilardi
Dina Waters as Tracy Montrose Blair

Jacob Vargas as Paco
Lombardo Boyar as Powerful
Karmin Murcelo as Paco's Mother
Tony Perez as Paco's Father
Candy Brown-Houston as Detective McBride
Dean Norris as Detective Shea
Armando Valdes as Luis
Elizabeth Rodriguez as Sylvie
Mary-Pat Green as Priest
Ken Abraham as Bowling Buddy
Roger Velasco as Young Man with Tattoos
Jim Ryan as A/C Repairman
Blaine Pate as Redneck
Luis Robledo as Rival

WHO'S THE STIFF?

Manuel Pedro Antonio Bolin, 1980-2001: Known to his fellow gang members as 'Paco', Manuel Bolin's car breaks down in the middle of a rival gang's territory. Going to phone for help, Paco is surrounded by rival gang members and shot.

PLOT SUMMARY

The police interrogate Nate and Brenda about the fire at the abandoned house. Although the police have no evidence to directly link either of them to the incident, they still have their suspicions about Claire's involvement – particularly after her recent foot-stealing. Back at home, Nate voices his own fears to David and Ruth that Claire may have started the fire.

David and Nate then have an intake meeting with Paco's parents and his gang leader, Powerful. Powerful is determined that his gang member will have an expensive funeral, but Paco's parents don't want him to have anything to do with the arrangements. Sensing that trouble is building, David goes down to the preparation room and asks Rico if he will come and speak to Powerful. Rico is insulted by David's prejudice – he automatically assumed that because Rico is Hispanic he would be more likely to know how to deal with a gang leader. David apologises for jumping to conclusions, and Rico goes to speak to Powerful. He stands his ground with the overbearing gang leader, clearly stating that if he doesn't begin to support Paco's family's wishes, then Fisher & Sons won't go through with the burial – and practically every other funeral home has already turned this particularly dangerous group of mourners away. Chastened by Rico's words, Powerful agrees to abide by Mr and Mrs Bolin's wishes.

Later that day, David and Keith are loading up Keith's car with groceries from the supermarket when a man, keen to hurry them up and claim their parking space, calls them 'fucking fags'. Keith sees red and storms over to him. He rams his LAPD badge in the man's face and warns him that the next time he calls somebody a fag, he'd better make sure that 'fag' isn't on the LAPD. David is shocked by Keith's response and tells him that he overreacted.

Keith, in turn, is furious with David – he asks him if he really hates himself enough *not* to react to such an insult.

David returns to the prep room, where the late Paco chastises him for not understanding why Keith was so angry. Paco points out that the insult was aimed at them both – by not getting angry at the homophobic insult, David was not only demeaning himself, he was also demeaning the out and proud Keith.

Upstairs, Brenda has arrived a little early for a family dinner being hosted by Ruth. Nate shows her round the house, and in the slumber room the couple start to kiss. Ruth comes downstairs to tell them that dinner is ready, only to walk in on them whilst Nate is performing oral sex on Brenda. Ruth screams in horror and rushes back upstairs, leaving a shell-shocked Nate and Brenda to adjust their clothing and regain their composure. The subsequent meal is a bit of a disaster, with Ruth interrogating Brenda over her career and her lifestyle. Brenda's flippant responses leave Claire in fits of giggles and Ruth decidedly unimpressed.

During Paco's viewing the next day, David is surprised when Tracy Montrose Blair shows up. She tells him that she often goes to funerals of people she didn't know, but David is scared that she's trying to use that as an excuse to get to know him better. David firmly tells her that she isn't really welcome at this viewing and shows her the door. Meanwhile, Claire is smoking pot in the preparation room with Luis, one of Paco's fellow gang members. She tries to appear mature and grown up in front of him and flirts openly with the gangster. However, he sees her as a middle-class little girl and walks away. Upstairs, Ruth tells Nate some good news – the police have phoned and ruled that the cause of the house fire was 'unknown'. Despite this, Nate is still suspicious of his sister.

The next day at church, David and Keith make up following their argument. Keith accepts David's apology, but tells him that although he understands David's fear of coming out, he won't go back into the closet (passively accepting homophobic abuse, for instance) for anybody, not even David.

Later that day, Nate and David present Ruth with their proposals for the future of Fisher & Sons. They tell her that they need almost $100,000 to update the business, to make it competitive and to advertise for more customers, and they ask her to lend them the money out of Nathaniel's life insurance. Ruth surprises her sons by telling them that she will not lend them the money – instead, she will become an investor and shareholder in Fisher & Sons, and that she expects a fair rate of return for her investment!

Matthew Gilardi has asked for another meeting with Nate and David, in order to give them a final offer to buy out their business. David is scared of going to the meeting, and he asks Paco what *he* would do if his family was being bullied. Paco grabs David by the throat and threatens his life, in a scarily convincing fashion. At the meeting, Gilardi goes into his usual routine of bullying and threats until David turns the tables on him, not literally threatening his life, but instead promising that there are much worse things that could happen to Gilardi than losing his life… Gilardi is shocked and quickly leaves. A stunned and delighted Nate congratulates his brother on his bravery, but David suddenly begins to feel nauseous as the reality of what he's just done sinks in.

Brenda brings a present to Ruth to make up for embarrassing her. Ruth accepts the basket of expensive bath products and Brenda's apology, beginning to like the young woman. Shortly after, Powerful arrives at Fisher & Sons to thank Rico and the Fishers for their help and to conduct a short prayer service for the souls of Paco and Nathaniel.

That night, David and Keith go bowling. David makes a break-through in acknowledging his relationship with Keith when a group of men ask if they are together, and he answers 'yes'. At Brenda's house, Nate suddenly has a horrible realisation. Brenda has filled the room with candles – this sudden interest in fire, combined with the still unexplained tattoo of 'Nathaniel' on her back, makes Nate wonder if Brenda did indeed start the fire out of an obsessive love for him.

At home, Ruth asks Claire straight out if she started the fire. She says no, but admits that she may have taken the foot…

THE PRODIGAL SON

Nate suffers the ultimate embarrassment and humiliation in 'Familia' – not only getting caught by your mother having sex, but being caught having unconventional sex in the middle of a funeral home during daylight hours. It's to Nate's credit that despite this mortifying moment, he still respects his mother's wishes and attends her family dinner. Nate at heart doesn't want to continually wind up in trouble – indeed, when being interrogated by the police, he downplays what actually occurred between him and Brenda in the abandoned house (unlike Brenda, who goes into explicit detail!) However, his love of exciting and risky behaviour will lead to him getting caught out in similar circumstances in the not too distant future. Furthermore, when he puts two and two together and realises that Brenda could be the arsonist, he doesn't do what most ordinary people would do and run away screaming, he stays to find out if his hunch is correct. To Nate, life is nothing if you can't feel the flame…

ANAL CONTROL FREAK

In 'Familia', David is forced to face up to his responsibilities: he is in a relationship, and as such he is expected to stand up to anyone who insults or attacks his partner. By not saying anything, David is admitting that he is no better than the 'fag' he gets called. It takes David's 'conversation' with Paco (during which he imagines what the gang leader would do under similar circumstances) for him to stand up for himself, and it's the slimy Gilardi who finds himself on the wrong end of David's genuinely scary threats. This surge of self-confidence is a fantastic moment that gets the audience cheering for David – surely it can't be long before he has the strength of character to be able to come out completely?

MOMMY, DEAREST

Considering just how repressed and conservative Ruth is, she actually deals with the shock of walking in on her son going down on Brenda quite well. Yes, she screams and runs away, but she still maintains the façade of a happy family. And that's Ruth's strength (and biggest weakness): don't worry about addressing underlying problems, because as long as everything appears to be normal, that's fine. In many ways, it would probably have been a lot better for Ruth if she had lost her temper. However, her simmering dislike of Brenda is nipped in the bud by Brenda herself. By making the effort to apologise and eat humble pie, Brenda does the wisest thing she could possibly have done. Although Ruth doesn't have as much overt control over her children as she might wish, they still look up to her. When she agrees to invest in Fisher & Sons, this is Ruth's biggest ever admission that she loves, trusts and admires her children, even if she's still not able to say those words out loud without it sounding like emotional blackmail.

TEENAGE KICKS

By now, we should be used to watching Claire flirt around unsuitable young men, but her attempted seduction of gang member Luis takes things to a far scarier level. Thankfully for Claire's long-term health, Luis can see through her bluster to the truth – she is no more than a scared little middle-class white girl who's desperate to fit in. When Luis rejects her, it makes Claire re-evaluate her own perspective on life. She soon finds herself having a truthful conversation with her mother – something she would never even have contemplated a short time before.

DREAM ON, DREAMER

Almost all of the dream sequences in this episode concern David's conversations with Paco. Even David is taken aback by the advice that he ends up receiving, but the benefits seem to pay off almost straight away.

SOUNDTRACK

Shuggie Otis – 'Inspiration Information' (In the prep room, David asks for Rico's help)

Coinmonster – 'Body Of Binky' (Keith fights with David in the supermarket car park)
Tchaikovsky – 'Sleeping Beauty' (Ruth walks in on Nate and Brenda)
Mariachi All-Stars – 'Sufriendo A Solas' / Schubert – 'Ave Maria' (Paco's viewing)
Vivaldi – 'Four Seasons: Winter' (Tracy appears at Paco's viewing)
Donna Fargo – 'Happiest Girl In The Whole USA' (David and Nate's meeting with Gilardi)
Pete Yorn – 'Life On A Chain' (David and Keith go bowling)
The Herbaliser – 'A Mother For Your Mind' (Brenda and Nate together)

SEX, DRUGS AND ROCK 'N' ROLL

Claire shares a joint with Luis in the preparation room. Nate and Brenda continue their habit of having sex in places where they might be discovered – and on this occasion, Ruth walks in on their pre-dinner appetiser. Later on, they share yet another steamy encounter, this time by the flicker of candlelight.

THE BRIGHT SIDE OF DEATH

Detective Shea (investigating what happened in the abandoned house): Could you please be as specific as possible? Just to establish a timeline.
Brenda: Well, he went down on me for a while. He's really good at it.

David: One day... I will find you or someone you love... I'm not saying anyone's gonna die. There are tragedies far worse than death. Things you couldn't even dream of, you spineless candy-ass corporate fuck.

ISN'T THAT WHATSHISNAME?

Jacob Vargas (Paco)'s film credits include *Crimson Tide* (Tony Scott, 1995), *Get Shorty* (Barry Sonnenfeld, 1995), *Romy and Michele's High School Reunion* (David Mirkin, 1997), and *Traffic* (Steven Soderbergh, 2000). He also voiced little Pepito in *Dr Dolittle 2* (Steve Carr, 2001). **Lombardo Boyar** (Powerful) played Chuy in *The Bernie Mac Show* and Enrique in *Candyman 3: Day of the Dead*. **Dean Norris** (Detective Shea) played Father Jerry Downey in the first series of cop drama *NYPD Blue*. His film appearances include *The Lawnmower Man* (Brett Leonard, 1992), *The Firm* (Sydney Pollack, 1993), *The Last Seduction* (John Dahl, 1994), *The Negotiator* (F. Gary Gray, 1998), *The Cell* (Tarsem Singh, 2000) and *The One* (James Wong, 2001). **Tony Perez** (Paco's Father) played Officer Mike Perez in the groundbreaking TV show *Hill Street Blues* and made a cameo appearance in the film *Blow* (Ted Demme, 2001). Behind the camera, he was also the second assistant director on *Terminator 2: Judgment Day* (James Cameron, 1991). **Roger Velasco** (Young Man with Tattoos) appeared in *Power Rangers Turbo* as the Green Turbo Ranger and *Power Rangers in Space* as the Black Space Ranger.

UNANSWERED QUESTIONS

✝ Did Brenda really start the fire? Is she dangerously obsessed with Nate?
✝ If Brenda didn't start the fire, who did?
✝ Is this the last we'll see of Gilardi and Kroehner?
✝ Is Tracy Montrose Blair really stalking David?

EULOGY

Not an especially eventful episode plot-wise, 'Familia' instead concentrates on letting the audience into the hearts and minds of the characters. We finally begin to gain a bit of respect for David, a man who until now has veered between cowardice and stupidity in his dealings with family and friends. In 'Familia' he learns how every now and again it is right to stand up for the things you believe in, and that accepting it when people ride roughshod over you isn't the right way to go if you want to be happy in life. Brenda and Nate's relationship continues to develop in its own twisted way, too – but for the real story on how messed up Brenda's past has been, we need to wait until the next episode…

EPISODE 5
AN OPEN BOOK

Directed by: Kathy Bates
Written by: Alan Ball

GUEST CAST
Joanna Cassidy as Margaret Chenowith
Robert Foxworth as Bernard Chenowith
Tim Maculan as Father Jack
Dina Waters as Tracy Montrose Blair
David Norona as Gary Deitman (School Psychiatrist)

Veronica Hart as Viveca St John
Cristine Rose as Hannah
Jordan Ladd as Ginnie
Joyce Greenleaf as Mrs Murdoch
Terence Knox as Larry Wadd
Sandra Oh as Porn Starlet
Jessica Stone as Young Brenda
Timothy Lynn Greer as Man in Choir

WHO'S THE STIFF?

Jean Louise McArthur ('Viveca St John'), 1957- 2001: A middle-aged porn actress, who is accidentally electrocuted when her pet cat knocks her set of heated rollers into the bath in which she is relaxing.

PLOT SUMMARY

It's Sunday morning, and David goes to his old family church, St Bart's, with his mother. After the service, Father Jack approaches David and tells him how happy he is to see him back in the fold. David explains that he's been going to a different church lately – St Stephen's in West Hollywood. Father Jack raises an eyebrow, as if to imply he knows what kind of congregation attends St Stephen's. Father Jack tells Ruth and David that since Nathaniel's death, there has been a vacant deacon's position within the church, and suggests that David might want to consider being put forward for the role. David is flattered, and Ruth is thrilled by the honour. A few moments later, David is accosted once again by Tracy Montrose Blair. She flirts very badly with him, and goes away disappointed when David lies to her, telling her that he is actually engaged to be married.

Nate has been invited over by Brenda to see her parents' stunning mansion. As her parents are away for the weekend, Brenda and Nate waste no time enjoying a semi-clad embrace in the swimming pool. Of course, at that moment, Margaret and Bernard Chenowith return home. Brenda introduces her parents to her boyfriend. Margaret and Bernard appear totally unfazed by meeting Nate this way, and invite him to join them for dinner soon.

At the request of the school psychiatrist, Ruth joins Claire for one of her therapy sessions. He tries to get the pair to break down the barriers between themselves, but within a few short moments they are shouting and bitching at each other again. It seems that not even a qualified counsellor can help them. David has an intake meeting with a porn industry friend of Viveca's. David, unaware of his client's former profession, gets a rude awakening when Nate and Rico recognise Viveca from some of her movies. Rico faces another problem with Viveca's reconstruction: when she died in her bath, her breasts were hanging in different directions. Now that rigor mortis has set in, it will be very difficult to readjust them – a particularly tricky fact, considering that the dress she is to wear in her coffin will display her ample bosom to its greatest effect.

In an attempt to get to know her daughter, Ruth hires two family comedy videos to watch with her. Sadly, both Claire and Ruth hate the films, and once they turn the movies off, the pair start to row again. Meanwhile, David is at Keith's apartment, enjoying a Chinese meal and a night in front of the TV with his boyfriend. David tells Keith about the possibility of him becoming a deacon at St Bart's. Keith is pleased that David has been given such an honour, but is upset that they will no longer be able to go to church at St Stephen's together. They make an arrangement that they will spend the weekend at the Gay Firemen and Policemen's Club together.

Nate arrives for dinner at the Chenowith house, and is shocked and a little angry when he realises that Brenda won't be joining them for the meal – Bernard and Margaret's invitation was to Nate only, so that they could find out more about their daughter's new man. During the meal, Bernard and Margaret fill Nate in on a great deal of background information about Brenda. The 'Nathaniel' tattoo on Brenda's back comes from a series of books that she was passionate about reading when she was a child, *Nathaniel and Isabel*. Nate discovers that his girlfriend was a child genius with an IQ of 185 – her unusually precocious behaviour patterns were detailed in a book written by her psychiatrist Dr Gareth Feinberg, entitled *Charlotte: Light and Dark*. Reeling from the revelations, Nate goes to see Brenda, angry that he had to hear it from her parents. Brenda tells Nate that although she wanted him to know all about her, she was scared to reveal all the facts because of how he might judge her. Nate replies by telling Brenda that he wants their relationship to be more than purely physical – he wants their relationship to go much deeper. Thankfully, Brenda agrees.

Ruth's next attempt to improve the relationship with her daughter involves both of them spending the night at Ruth's cousin Hannah's house. Hannah has an amazingly close relationship with her daughter Ginnie, and Ruth hopes that some of their happiness will rub off on Claire and herself. However, as the night progresses, Ruth realises that Hannah and Ginnie are insufferably smug about their happiness, a happiness that is actually very shallow. Faced with the terrifying prospect of being forced to go to a spinning class (aerobics on an exercise bike) with their saccharine relatives, Ruth and Claire flee the house, giggling together as they go. Back home, the two women have their first proper heart-to-heart. Ruth confesses to Claire about her affair with Hiram. Claire is shocked, but listens to her mother pouring her heart out. Later, when talking to her school psychiatrist Gary Deitman, Claire bursts into tears, upset that she cannot help her mother through her sadness.

Nate and Brenda are having an early breakfast at a café when they see Keith and David eating together too. Seizing his moment at last, David takes Keith's hand, making a clear declaration to his brother about his sexuality. Nate is stunned, but takes the news very well, leaving with Brenda who comments that David is very lucky to be going out with somebody as 'hot' as Keith. Keith is really proud of David for having the courage to come out to his brother, but his happiness soon turns sour. David tells Keith that because of his new commitments at church, he won't be able to go away with him for the weekend. Keith is disappointed and suggests a compromise – they'll just go away for one night, then Keith can come with David to church on Sunday morning. David is clearly very uncomfortable with this suggestion and tells Keith no. Keith is furious at David. He calls him a coward, and the two of them split up.

At Brenda's house, Nate is shocked to discover a naked man walking around, with only a towel to cover his modesty. After a few moments of confusion and jealousy, he realises that this is Billy, Brenda's brother. As Billy turns around to get dressed, Nate notices a tattoo on the small of his back that reads 'Isabel' – a perfect match to Brenda's 'Nathaniel' tattoo.

At Viveca's viewing, Nate is amazed at how perfectly matched her breasts have become. Rico is very proud of his work, and tells Nate that he used a strategically placed can of cat food to position each breast. The service attracts a motley assortment of stars from the porn industry, shocking Ruth and scaring away two potential clients! The next Sunday, David is ordained as a deacon at St Bart's. After the service, he is congratulated by his whole family, who have turned up for his big day. However, Keith is nowhere to be seen.

THE PRODIGAL SON

Well, Nate has been hoping to find out more about his girlfriend Brenda for quite a while now, but surely even he never expected to discover so much about her in one deeply disturbing meal with her parents. He discovers that Brenda is a super-genius who spent much of her early life in therapy – indeed, she even had a book written about her case by one of her psychiatrists. As a result, Brenda has learnt how to play mind games with those who try to test her. Margaret and Bernard Chenowith suggest that Brenda could very well be playing games with Nate, but at this stage he chooses not to believe their cynical interpretation and to continue in a relationship that could potentially hurt him a great deal. By trusting Brenda, this notorious commitment-phobe is showing just how much he cares for this messed-up young woman. In return, she demonstrates her commitment to Nate by giving him a key to her house.

ANAL CONTROL FREAK

As Nate and Brenda's relationship strengthens, so David and Keith's falls apart. Although David takes a massive step towards accepting his own sexuality by finally coming out to his brother, he undoes all of this good work by re-immersing himself within a traditional Christian church, one that is unable to accept or validate his relationship. It's quite hard to understand why David really wants to volunteer for this job, knowing that it would undoubtedly place some strain on his relationship. His excuse that it might bring more business to Fisher & Sons is just that – an excuse. What's more likely is that David desperately feels as though he needs to make up in some way for being born gay – by investing additional time and effort into the church, his subconscious probably hopes to make amends for his sin.

MOMMY, DEAREST & TEENAGE KICKS

A huge leap forward takes place in this episode in Ruth's relationship with Claire and her ability to recover from Nathaniel's death. Ruth's attempts to show Claire a 'real' family fail hilariously as they realise that their own warring relationship is far more real than anything Hannah and Ginnie might pretend to have. As a result,

Ruth stops trying to force Claire into behaving in the way Ruth would wish her to behave – and realises that any relationship, even one with your youngest child, must eventually centre around mutual respect and communication. Ruth and Claire both acknowledge that they will probably never see eye to eye on most things, but in 'An Open Book' they make the first moves towards understanding each other's points of view – their relationship isn't perfect, but as long as they are open and honest with each other, they will be able to handle whatever life throws at them.

DREAM ON, DREAMER

David has lots of conversations with Viveca – she quizzes him on whether or not he finds her sexy, and then has a debate with him about the morality of her (and of course, by association, his own) lifestyle. As David faces the congregation at church, he imagines Viveca, dressed in a Marilyn Monroe-style outfit, blowing him a kiss from the middle of pews filled with naked men. Nate dreams of Brenda as a young girl, standing in front of some water, in a recreation of the cover of the book *Charlotte: Light and Dark*. The young girl changes into Brenda as she appears today, before turning and running away. I wonder what fear of abandonment *that* could represent?

SOUNDTRACK

Bobbie Gentry – 'Fancy' (Viveca is electrocuted)
Six Feet Under Choir – 'Oh For A Closer Walk With God' (David spots a handsome man in the choir)
Mozart – 'Dove Sonno' from *The Marriage of Figaro* (Nate arrives at the Chenowiths')
Puccini – 'Humming Chorus' from *Madam Butterfly* (Dinner with the Chenowiths)
Cowboy Junkies – 'A Common Disaster' (Nate meets Billy)
Vivaldi – 'Concerto #3 In G Major For Violin' (Viveca St John's viewing)

Mozart – 'Divertimento In D Major For Strings' (Porn starlet interrupts David)

SEX, DRUGS AND ROCK 'N' ROLL

Just the two examples of network-unfriendly behaviour in this week's episode. Firstly, Viveca St John's two notable assets make many appearances throughout the episode, causing much merriment for Rico and Nate. And secondly, it just wouldn't feel like an episode of *Six Feet Under* without a Nate and Brenda moment – this week, they're having a bit of fun splashing around in a swimming pool when Bernard and Margaret Chenowith turn up. This getting interrupted mid-shag is becoming a bit of a habit for them…

THE BRIGHT SIDE OF DEATH

Brenda: Nate, these are my parents, Margaret and Bernard Chenowith. Margaret and Bernard, this is Nate Fisher, the man I am having sex with.
Margaret: Hello! Brenda has told us absolutely nothing about you…

Nate: This is Brenda, my er … my girlfriend.
Brenda: I prefer the term 'fuck puppet'.

Porn Starlet: I met her on *Deep Diving*. (Audience claps politely) Thank you. And I had never gone down on a girl before, so, naturally, I was nervous, but Viveca was so warm and relaxed about it. She really put me at ease. Well, her and the two Xanex she gave me.

ISN'T THAT WHATSHISNAME?

Robert Foxworth (Bernard Chenowith) has had a very successful TV career, most notably playing Chase Gioberti in prime-time soap *Falcon Crest* from 1981-1987. He also made a memorable guest appearance in *Star Trek: Deep Space Nine* as Admiral Leyton and was in the movie *City of Angels* playing Dr Dan Prince. Similarly, **Joanna Cassidy** (Margaret Chenowith) has had her fair share of major TV work, including appearing opposite Robert Foxworth in *Falcon Crest* as Katherine Demery, as well as shows like *Dallas*, *Diagnosis Murder* and *The District*. She's also appeared in many movies, notably *Blade Runner* (Ridley Scott, 1982) and *Who Framed Roger Rabbit* (Robert Zemeckis,1988).

Veronica Hart (Viveca St John) was a real-life respected porn star of the 70s and 80s who went on to take minor roles in more mainstream movies. She retired from performing (sexually) in adult movies in the mid 80s and was nominated for Best Adult Film Director in 2001 by the Adult Video News (AVN) Award 2002 Show. **Sandra Oh** (Porn Starlet) has appeared in the movie *Bean* and TV shows including *Judging Amy* and *Arli$$*, as well as playing Rita Wu in *Further Tales of the City*. **Cristine Rose** (Hannah) has been seen in bit parts in *Star Trek: The Next Generation*, *Grace Under Fire* and *Providence*. **Jordan Ladd** (Ginnie) is the daughter of ex-Charlie's Angel Cheryl Ladd and the granddaughter of famous movie star Alan Ladd. **Terence Knox** (Larry Wadd) is probably best known in the UK for his regular roles as Dr Peter White in *St Elsewhere* and as Sergeant Zeke Anderson in *Tour of Duty*. **Jessica Stone** (Young Brenda) had a small role in Ang Lee's *The Ice Storm* (1997).

UNANSWERED QUESTIONS

✟ In the pilot episode, Brenda told Nate that her parents own an 'ancient Springer Spaniel', but we do not see him in this episode. Where is he?

EULOGY

Probably the warmest and funniest episode of the first season of *Six Feet Under*, 'An Open Book' nevertheless takes us on a journey to a very dark place as for the first time we get to see exactly what kind of a background Brenda Chenowith has. Brenda's bizarre childhood of therapy and intellectual game-playing is a huge concept for Nate to try to take in. However, it does begin to answer a lot of questions about her behaviour that have been worrying him, and opening up about who she is (and literally opening up by giving Nate a key to her house) helps to solidify their relationship. Other characters who act in a more open fashion make great leaps forward in their relationships too – Claire and Ruth start to talk to each other for the first time, and David finally manages to come out to his brother. However, another pairing falls apart – David and Keith split up, largely because of David's decision to become a deacon at the traditionalist church of St Bart's.

In short, the message of this episode is that honesty is *always* the best policy – even if the short-term effects of this honesty are painful and upsetting. In the long run, no relationship will survive without being honest to your partner and, just as importantly, to yourself.

EPISODE 6
THE ROOM

Directed by: Rodrigo Garcia
Written by: Christian Taylor

GUEST CAST
Ed Begley Jr as Hiram
Richard Jenkins as Nathaniel
Ed O'Ross as Nikolai
Tim Maculan as Father Jack
Dina Waters as Tracy Montrose Blair

Bill Cobbs as Mr Jones
Shishir Kurup as Restaurant Owner
Jeff Corbett as David's One-Night Stand (Greg Clarkson)
Tim de Zarn as Mechanic
Lorinne Vozoff as Jessica Wilcox
David Stifel as Indigent Man
Howard Mungo as Man at Viewing
Jessica Stone as Young Brenda

WHO'S THE STIFF?

Mildred 'Hattie' Effinger Jones, 1922-2001: An elderly lady who passed away quietly in her sleep.

PLOT SUMMARY

At Brenda's house, Nate begins to read *Charlotte: Light and Dark*, hoping to get an insight into his girlfriend. She's uncomfortable with him reading 'that shit' and briefly has a flashback to the type of psychological cross-examination she went through as a child. She heads off for work, giving Nate a lift. Ruth is trying to decide what to do with her day – she plans to reorganise the cupboards in her kitchen. Both David and Claire walk past Ruth as she stands in the kitchen, strangely immobile.

David conducts an induction meeting with Mr Jones. He's quite snappy and angry towards David, plainly deeply upset at losing his wife. David is very patient with the stubborn old man, even agreeing to waive the standard fee for embalming so that he can view his wife one last time.

Nate goes to collect his car, which has been in the garage for servicing. He's surprised when the mechanic tells him he doesn't need to pay. Apparently, some years ago, Nathaniel buried the mechanic's brother and essentially 'traded the funeral for oil changes'. Nate is intrigued and decides to do some further investigating. He goes through Nathaniel's old ledgers and notices a red asterisk next to the funeral conducted for the mechanic's brother. Going through the file, Nate sees a number of other funerals also marked with an asterisk, and decides to go and speak to each of the families of those his father buried, intent on trying to find out why his father decided to barter the funerals rather than accept payment as normal.

On Sunday morning at church, David and Ruth are approached by Tracy Montrose Blair, who links arms with David in yet another over-friendly way. She questions him again about his fiancée, but Ruth unwittingly lets the cat out of the bag and says, 'What fiancée?' At that point, Hiram Gundarsson arrives to speak with Ruth. David is deeply unhappy to see 'the hairdresser', but Ruth seems quite glad to renew her acquaintance.

Meanwhile, Mr Jones practically forces his way into Fisher & Sons to see his wife, despite the fact that nobody is there to help him. Claire explains that he can wait for David and Nate to get home if he wishes. Brenda, who has called by to see if Nate can lend her a hand moving a chest of drawers she's just bought, ends up with Claire as a volunteer instead. At Brenda's, Claire meets Billy and is instantly smitten by him. She's practically gobsmacked to discover that Brenda actually is Charlotte from *Charlotte: Light and Dark*, a book that Claire and her friends were obsessed about three years earlier. 'Oh my God! It's like meeting Gandhi! Or Jesus!' she exclaims. Brenda notices that Billy is flirting with the very young Claire and offers to take her home, but Billy offers Claire a lift instead, and she naturally accepts the lift from the handsome young man. As Billy drops Claire off at home, they kiss. She warns him not to mess with her, and he promises that he's not trying to use her.

Nate is visiting the customers in his father's ledger marked with an asterisk. He's somewhat taken aback to discover just how loved Nathaniel was by so many people. They describe him in affectionate terms like 'kook' and many are deeply upset to discover that they won't be seeing Nathaniel again. Nate is even more astonished when he finds out what services Nathaniel had bartered in exchange for a funeral – a regular monthly supply of pot from horticulturalist Jessica Wilcox, and most strangely, a dingy room behind a restaurant. Nate discovers that Nathaniel used the room for seven years, visiting it on an irregular basis – sometimes every day, sometimes not for months. Nate ponders what on earth his father could have used the room for. The room contains a sofa, a record player, a table and chairs and a TV, and that's about it.

David helps out with the food distribution programme for the homeless and is stuck between the chattering Tracy Montrose Blair and his mother's bit on the side, Hiram. He snubs all attempts by Hiram to make the peace between them, and tries his best to ignore Tracy's clumsy flirting. In the end, he's forced to hurt Tracy's feelings to get her to leave him alone. He tells her to do them both a favour and go to a bar and pick somebody up – he's not interested. On his way home, David drives past a West Hollywood gay club and stares longingly at a couple kissing in the road in front of him.

At home, Ruth gets her regular delivery from one of her husband's flower suppliers, Nikolai. She thanks Nikolai for not abandoning Fisher & Sons because of pressure from Kroehner, but is slightly alarmed by his over-familiarity. Later that night, Ruth decides to clean all of her cupboards out. She's shocked to discover a jar of fifteen-year-old baby food at the very back. It brings back how much time has elapsed in her life. When Nikolai delivers yet more flowers the next day for Mrs Jones' funeral, Ruth's even more disturbed by the 'sex look' he keeps giving her. Ruth tells Nikolai to stop looking at her in that way, but when Nikolai says that maybe she likes it, Ruth slaps him hard across the face. Still smiling, Nikolai leaves. Mr Jones, who's overheard the whole conversation, tells Ruth that she needs to get laid!

Nate brings Brenda to see his father's mystery room. She's just as intrigued as he is, but is happy to accept that perhaps Nathaniel just wanted to have a space that was his and nobody else's. Nate tells her that he doesn't want to be the kind of person who dies and people say they didn't know what he was really like.

Billy arrives at school to collect Claire. He takes photos of her at school, and then back at her home. He even sets the camera on timer before kissing her and fondling her breast just as the photograph is taken. When Claire tells Billy that she thinks Nate is really in love with Brenda, Billy suddenly goes colder and walks out, telling her that they will have to do it again sometime.

David decides to go to a club and is picked up by a handsome man who takes him back to his apartment. David lies to the young man and says he's a lawyer from Boston called Jim. He's rather uncomfortable about the situation, but seems happy to finally have found someone simply to have sex with. David doesn't spend the night there and drives home as soon as he's finished having sex.

The next day, Ruth apologises to Nikolai for hitting him. As she's explaining about being surrounded by 'relics of a life that no longer exists', Nikolai leans in and kisses her. She doesn't push him away. However, Claire is conclusively pushed away by Billy. She phones him up to see if he wants to meet up with her after school, but he tells her no, he doesn't. 'What do you think I am, a paedophile?' Billy hangs up on her, leaving Claire stunned and very angry. After school, Brenda arrives to speak with Claire. She explains that although she loves Billy very much, he's a very confused and mixed-up man, and that she feels sorry for whoever ends up with him.

Nate takes David to see his father's room. David is quite dismissive about it and tells Nate that people are allowed to have a private life. When Nate tries to convince David that it's important for the family to be honest with each other, David retorts that he thinks Nate won't be happy until the whole family is in therapy. Nate starts to clear his father's belongings out of the room. Whilst he's doing so, he discovers an old photograph album, showing pictures of the whole family. He finds some Polaroid photos of his semi-nude mother, which he takes back home to show her. She's entranced by them. She explains to Nate that Nathaniel took them just before he went away to Vietnam – he even kept them in his pocket throughout the war to protect him.

Nate goes downstairs and discovers Mr Jones still sitting with his late wife, as he has been for the past few days. However, on closer inspection, Nate realises that Mr Jones has actually died whilst sitting there, reunited with his beloved Hattie. After her family have gone to bed, Ruth surprises Hiram by turning up unannounced on his doorstep. They kiss, passionately.

THE PRODIGAL SON

Nate's attempt to discover why his father wanted him to be a part of the family business gets bogged down in yet more surprise revelations in this episode. With the discovery of the secret room, he is forced to face the fact that he will never really know what his father was like. As 'Nathaniel' points out to him, if he had so many questions, why did he never bother asking them whilst he was alive? As a well-balanced Libran, Nate feels as though everything in life really should have balance and should make some kind of sense. It's Brenda, the free spirit, who has to point out to Nate that sometimes things just don't work out like that.

ANAL CONTROL FREAK

After many weeks of trying to let Tracy down gently, David finds himself forced into a corner and unable to make it clear that he's not interested in her. David lashes out at Tracy and hurts her feelings, but as she's so clueless you almost feel that it's the only way he could ever get the message across to her. However, Tracy has hit the nail on the head – David is indeed lonely and needs the comfort of somebody. He turns to picking up a man in a club and going home with him, but it's clear that this encounter is only helping with the short-term physical need – it's never going to make him happy or replace the stability of his relationship with Keith.

MOMMY, DEAREST

It's taken a long time for Ruth to realise that her life must move forward, but in 'The Room' she takes decisive action about making her life more complete. Until now, Ruth has sublimated her pain and mourning and has devoted her energies into trying to ensure that her family is happy. When Nikolai makes a pass at her, Ruth realises that her life need not be empty. Seeing the photographs of herself as a beautiful young woman makes her realise that death has always surrounded her. Nathaniel took those photos as he went off to fight in the Vietnam War, and there was always a very real chance that he might never come back. Ruth now realises that every day could be *her* last – there's no point in wasting her life away by being too scared to live it. With two potential suitors to choose from, it's no real surprise that Ruth decides to renew her affair with Hiram. He's intelligent, cultured and cares for Ruth deeply. The crude, base overtures of Nikolai are something that Ruth is just not prepared to accept yet.

TEENAGE KICKS

Yet again, Claire gets her fingers burned when dabbling with romance. She tries to force Billy into behaving in a fashion that will ensure that she isn't hurt, but is consequently completely floored when he changes his attitude towards her overnight. Brenda is thankfully there to explain about Billy's unpredictable behaviour, but being treated in such a cavalier fashion might almost be enough to persuade Claire to give up on love for ever (or at least for the foreseeable future!) It's great to see Claire and Brenda bonding so well, as the two of them really do have a great deal in common – not just their brothers or *Charlotte: Light and Dark*, either!

DREAM ON, DREAMER

We get flashbacks to two of Brenda's early memories – one of her undergoing psychoanalysis by Dr Feinberg and claiming that he raped her doll, and another of her refusing to co-operate with him by barking in response to his questioning.

Nate pictures a vast array of different activities that Nathaniel might have gotten up to in his secret room – from having sex with prostitutes, to smoking dope, to using a giant bong with bikers, to even using a rifle to recreate the JFK assassination. Nate later speaks to 'Nathaniel' and tries to clear up a few more questions he still wants the answers to.

SOUNDTRACK

Amboy Dukes – 'Journey To The Center Of The Mind' (Nate dreams of his father's life)

Classics 4 – 'Spooky' (Nate talks to his father's ghost)

Spylab – 'Celluloid Hypnotic (Hypnotic Remix)' (David drives past a gay club)

Chris Walsh and Dave Beran – 'Shake' (David goes into the gay club)

Craig Armstrong – 'Let's Go Out Tonight' (Closing moments)

SEX, DRUGS AND ROCK 'N' ROLL

Nate discovers his father's marijuana use, and later imagines Nathaniel using a huge bong to get a bigger hit from the pot. We also see Claire and Brenda smoking a joint together. There's not much on-screen sex, but David gets lucky and Ruth decides to rekindle her romance with Hiram. Claire can count herself lucky that she didn't go all the way with Billy, considering how quickly she got dumped and his rapid mood-swings afterwards.

THE BRIGHT SIDE OF DEATH

Claire (talking about Mr Jones): I helped him sit down. Then I had to listen to him bitch and moan about public transportation for fucking *ever*, and then he just, like, passed out. Now I can't get his fucking hand to let go!
Brenda: Maybe he died.
Claire: Very funny. No, he's still breathing. And farting.

Jones: (from next room) Lady wear red, she means business.
Ruth: This is just what was clean.
Jones: Lady, I can see you from here, and I'm blind and deaf. You need to get yourself laid.

ISN'T THAT WHATSHISNAME?

Ed O'Ross (Nikolai) has appeared in many hugely successful films, including *Lethal Weapon* (Richard Donner, 1987) *Full Metal Jacket* (Stanley Kubrick, 1987) as Lieutenant Walter J. 'Touchdown' Tinoshky, *Dick Tracy* (Warren Beatty, 1990) as Itchy, and *Universal Soldier* (Roland Emmerich, 1992) as Colonel Perry. **Shishir Kurup** (Restaurant Owner) was a semi-regular anaesthesiologist in TV series *Chicago Hope* and is a founder member of the Cornerstone Theater Company, which establishes local theatre groups across the USA. **Tim de Zarn** (Mechanic) can be seen in *Fight Club* (David Fincher, 1999), *Gone in Sixty Seconds* (Dominic Sena, 2000) and *Spider-Man* (Sam Raimi, 2002). **Lorinne Vozoff** (Jessica Wilcox) played authoritarian characters in both *L.A. Law* and *Party of Five*. **David Stifel** (Indigent Man) pops up in *A Life Less Ordinary* (Danny Boyle, 1997) and *Minority Report* (Steven Spielberg, 2002).

UNANSWERED QUESTIONS

✝ Is this the start of a beautiful new romance for Ruth and Hiram?
✝ Why did Billy dump Claire so brutally?

EULOGY

Perhaps the most important thing that many of the characters try to do in this episode is attempt to bring love into their lives: Claire with Billy, Ruth with Hiram and David with the one-night stand. Sadly, not all of them are successful. Still, at least they are making an effort to move their lives forward, whereas Nate is still struggling to come to terms with his current position. He looks for answers from the lifestyle his father lived – but without a real live person there to speak to, he's never going to be able to find those answers.

There's not much comfort either from the story of Mr and Mrs Jones. They spent their entire lives devoted to each other, with little room in their lives for anybody or anything else. When Mrs Jones dies, Mr Jones literally has nothing left to live for and dies himself. The cautionary tale we're presented with here tells us that yes, finding love is crucially important for anybody's happiness, but that love needs to be in proportion and to be a love that doesn't smother or overwhelm.

EPISODE 7
BROTHERHOOD

Directed by: Jim McBride
Written by: Christian Williams

GUEST CAST
Ed O'Ross as Nikolai
Tim Maculan as Father Jack
David Norona as Gary Deitman (School Psychiatrist)
Frank Birney as Walter Kriegenthaler
Marina Black as Parker McKenna
Nancy Linehan as Connie

Wade Andrew Williams as Paul Kovitch
Raphael Sbarge as Father Clark
Brian Kimmet as Victor Kovitch
Eric Ware as VA Administrator
Davis Henry as Private Bailey
Gary Murphy as Mooning Private
David McSwain as Vet in Wheelchair
George Pena as Flag Folder
Ange Billman as Parker's Friend (with baby)
Shannon Convery as Parker's Friend (with ovarian cancer)
Dianna Miranda as Bride
Luke Sabre as Private in Porno
Keith Amos as MP #1 in Porno
Raphael Gamon as MP #2 in Porno

WHO'S THE STIFF?

Victor Wayne Kovitch, PFC: 1971-2001: Thirty-year-old army veteran who died in his sleep after suffering from Gulf War Syndrome for many years.

PLOT SUMMARY

Early morning at Brenda's house, and Nate complains to her about how tired he's feeling. He feels that David is giving him all of the rubbish jobs to do – for instance, he spent the previous night driving a body to San Jose. Nate calls David to give him a piece of his mind, but David points out that until Nate passes the funeral directors' test, he cannot do anything else. Nate decides he needs the weekend off, and persuades Brenda into coming away with him to the Two Bunch Palms resort in the desert. Brenda and Nate enjoy an energetic sex session, but are interrupted when Billy walks in on them *in flagrante*. Nate is furious at yet another invasion of his and Brenda's privacy, and even Brenda isn't impressed by her brother's behaviour. However, she agrees to help him prepare for his upcoming art show. Nate heads off to collect yet another body for Fisher & Sons.

At the next deacons' meeting, the discussion centres on the appointment of an associate priest for St Bart's, Father Clark. The decision on whether or not to employ Father Clark seems to be split along 'traditional' and 'liberal' lines, with stubborn traditionalist Walter Kriegenthaler loudly voicing his concern that David was only asked to become a deacon so that Father Jack could swing the voting around to his own liberal tendencies. David decides to play things by the book and tells the rest of the deacons that he wishes to interview Father Clark personally before making his mind up.

Nate goes home to find David already conducting the intake meeting with Victor's brother Paul Kovitch. Nate knew Paul from high school where he was a wrestling champion, but there's not much celebration when Paul tells the Fishers that he wants Vic to be cremated with minimal fuss or ceremony. Paul informs them that Vic hated the army because of the Gulf War Syndrome he developed. Instead of the full military funeral that Vic is entitled to, Paul insists that his brother will have a small-scale civilian service. Later, David and Nate have an argument over who's going to collect Victor's body. David orders Nate to collect it, but Nate informs his brother that he's going to be taking the weekend off. David is furious and tells Nate that he can't possibly take time off right now. Ruth interrupts the boys' argument with the news that Hiram is coming over for dinner that night and that she expects them both to attend. Nate agrees, providing he can bring Brenda along.

After talking back to the teacher in her maths class at school, Claire goes to see the school psychiatrist Gary Deitman again. He has faith in Claire's ability, and tells her that if she concentrated she could literally ace her classes in algebra. Claire simply isn't interested in a subject that she perceives as irrelevant to her life. Dietman suggests that Claire may benefit from going on the Sierra Crossroads Programme – an outward bound course over the school's spring break that lets participants mountain climb, hike and get in touch with nature and themselves. Claire seems quite interested.

Later that same day, Ruth goes over to Nikolai's flower shop. She notices the 'Now Hiring' sign in the window and asks Nikolai if she can have a job. Nikolai is delighted to have 'Ruthie' around and agrees to let her work there. Meanwhile, David interviews Father Clark for the vacant position at St Bart's. Clark comes across as a very intelligent, fiercely sincere man who is determined that the deeply cynical and lazy congregation should get shaken up a bit. David is very impressed by Clark's passion for a modern and inclusive church.

Whilst they're examining Victor's body, Nate and Rico discover army medals taped to his chest. They check his records and discover that Vic had actually requested to be buried at the National Cemetery. Nate investigates at Vic's last hospital, and discovers that Vic was actually very proud indeed of his former army past, but was too afraid to tell his brother that he wanted to be buried as a national hero.

Ruth's dinner goes quite well, despite David and Claire's fantasies of what Hiram and Ruth's sex life may be like. Nate goes back home with Brenda where they discover a gift basket left for them by Billy, as an apology for walking in on them earlier. The basket is somewhat risqué, consisting of oysters, fruit, champagne, condoms and a large dildo. Nate's angry at yet another invasion of privacy, but Brenda assures him that Billy's mind just works on a different wavelength to most people.

Whilst David is at home watching a porn movie (ironically of a group of soldiers getting it on!), Walter Kriegenthaler phones him. Walter tells David that he thinks Father Clark might be gay – and as such, he is an unsuitable candidate to work at St Bart's. The next morning, Nate comes over to speak to David and lets him know that he's found out that Vic's ashes can indeed be buried at the National Cemetery. David is embarrassed beyond belief when Nate turns on the TV and sees the porn film that David had been watching the night before. Nate just laughs it off, telling his brother that he watches porn too!

At school, Claire is preparing to take her SATs (college entrance exams). She briefly talks to Parker McKenna, one of the most popular girls in class. She wishes Parker and her two friends well for the exams. However, Claire cannot concentrate on the exams and fills in her multiple-choice paper with a skull-and-crossbones design.

At the next meeting of St Bart's deacons, David casts the deciding vote in the question of Clark's employment – and votes *against* him joining the parish, presumably in order to convince his fellow deacons of his traditionalist morals and values. Ruth, meanwhile, is thoroughly enjoying her first day working at Nikolai's flower shop. In fact, she's so happy that Nikolai finds her crying her eyes out. Ruth explains that until today, she's associated the smell of flowers with mourning and grief – she's delighted that she's able to be around happy people for a change.

Vic's memorial service at Fisher & Sons goes well, with lots of his former comrades attending. Paul, however, is livid that there's been any army involvement whatsoever. He gets even more annoyed when one of Vic's former colleagues thanks him for allowing the military burial to take place. Nate explains to Paul about the information he discovered – a military burial was exactly what Vic really wanted. Paul, somewhat reluctantly, agrees to follow Vic's final wishes.

At Vic's burial, Nate and David agree that they want to have a closer relationship than Vic and Paul ever had. They hug and say how much they love each other – despite their bickering. That night, Nate heads over to Brenda's house to collect her for their weekend away. However, Brenda's house is a terrible mess. Billy is there and looks as if he's having a nervous breakdown of some sort. He is surrounded by hundreds and hundreds of his photographs, scattered all around Brenda's house in a seemingly random fashion. Brenda explains to Nate that Billy has stopped taking his medication and as such he's in no fit state to look after himself. Billy has come over to get Brenda to help him choose the photographs for his next show. He tells Nate that Brenda can't go away with him – 'You can fuck her some other time.' Nate leaves for his weekend away on his own, frustrated by the control that Billy has over Brenda.

THE PRODIGAL SON

Nate's really beginning to struggle with his current responsibilities towards Fisher & Sons. He's working silly hours, doing the menial tasks, and getting some terrible headaches as a result. He wants to have a fairer share of the work, but David just isn't able to let Nate deal with the sensitive side of the business until he passes his funeral directors' exam. So with things not going well at work, Nate turns to Brenda for support. It's been looming for a while now, but when he finally tells Brenda that he loves her, it's a big step for both of them. She's surprised by his admission and appears to almost take a step back from their relationship as a result. Does Brenda decide to stay at home to look after Billy, or is she staying at home to avoid committing herself to her boyfriend? When Brenda and Nate argue about her decision to stay behind, she stuns him with an enigmatic comment about fucking her brother. Just how twisted *is* Brenda's relationship with Billy?

ANAL CONTROL FREAK

David finally makes great strides in healing the damaged relation-ship with his brother Nate. Seeing the lack of communication between Paul and Victor Kovitch and the enmity that it left follow-ing Vic's death, David realises that he needs to forgive and forget. When the two brothers finally admit how much they love each other, it's a beautiful moment. However, in the rest of his life, David's behaviour goes from bad to worse. He deliberately votes against Father Clark in order to protect his own closeted status, despite the fact that there is no actual evidence to prove that Clark is gay. If he's not careful, David's going to end up so far back in the closet that he'll bump into a lion and a witch...

MOMMY, DEAREST

Ruth gets round to telling her family about her new relationship with Hiram and her new job at Nikolai's shop, and it's gratifying to see that most of them accept her new life. In fact, one of the few people to express a reservation about her job is Hiram. Ruth may be at risk of swapping her newfound freedom for a relationship that's even more restricting than her one with Nathaniel.

DREAM ON, DREAMER

Hiram's new relationship with Ruth causes both David and Claire to imagine astonishingly explicit interpretations of their mother's sex life. In particular, David's visualisation of Ruth stroking Hiram's crotch and saying 'I can't get enough of this cock!' is so beautifully out of character as to be hysterically funny.

Claire gets two other dream sequences, though – firstly imagining her maths teacher's head exploding (a bit of a running theme with Claire, this – did she see the movie *Scanners* by David Cronenberg when she was young?), then getting a glimpse into possible future lives for Parker and her friends.

SOUNDTRACK

EMF – 'Unbelievable' (In the background of Victor's video letter)

Victoria Williams – 'Water To Drink (Agua de Beber)' (Nate and Brenda flirt)

Vivaldi – 'Flute Concerto In G Major'/Vivaldi – 'Concerto In F Major' (The family dinner)

Darren Elpant – 'The Pump' (Porn movie soundtrack)

SEX, DRUGS AND ROCK 'N' ROLL

Brenda and Nate's rather acrobatic session is an eye-opener – particularly to Billy, who gets an eyeful himself. He later gives Brenda and Nate a basketful of goodies to help them improve their next session. Tasteful...

THE BRIGHT SIDE OF DEATH

Psychiatrist: Hey, have you heard of the Sierra Crossroads Programme?
Claire: What is that? Like, 'Bungee Jumping for Jesus'?

Ruth (tearful and confused): Today, I helped people choose flowers for weddings, for anniversaries, for new babies. I can't remember being surrounded by so much happiness.
Nikolai: Do not worry. We get funerals too.

ISN'T THAT WHATSHISNAME?

Marina Black (Parker McKenna) is the niece of Shirley Temple Black (the married name of former child star Shirley Temple). She played a hostage in the movie *Swordfish* (Dominic Sena, 2001). **Frank Birney** (Walter Kriegenthaler) appeared in TV show *The Practice* as Judge Warren West. **Wade Andrew Williams** (Paul Kovitch) made memorable guest appearances in *Buffy the Vampire*

Slayer as General Gregor, the leader of a group of holy knights combating hell goddess Glory, and in the fantastic *24* as doomed New Orleans-based informant Robert Ellis. He was also in *Erin Brockovich* (Steven Soderbergh, 2000) as one of the claimants that Erin supports. **Raphael Sbarge** (Father Clark) had a guest role in *Star Trek: Voyager*. **Gary Murphy** (Mooning Private) had a blink-and-you'll-miss-him role in the first episode of *24* as Kim Bauer's ex-boyfriend Vincent.

UNANSWERED QUESTIONS

✝ Are Nate's headaches really caused by overwork and exposure to formaldehyde fumes?

✝ Is Brenda and Billy's close relationship *really* incestuous?

EULOGY

Considering how much bitching and sniping we've seen between David and Nate Fisher, it's about time they put their differences behind them and started working together. As often happens, it's the effect of seeing the damaged relationship of another pair of brothers that makes them readdress their own dealings with each other. It's great to see Ruth finally making a life for herself, too – but will she be able to balance her new work and her new romance, or will she end up having to choose one over the other?

EPISODE 8
CROSSROADS

Directed by: Allen Coulter
Written by: Laurence Andries

GUEST CAST
Ed O'Ross as Nikolai
Marina Black as Parker
Steven Pasquale as Kurt
Garrison Hershberger as Matthew Gilardi
Justina Machado as Vanessa Diaz
Giancarlo Rodriguez as Julio Diaz

Stewart Finlay-McLennan as Connor
Michael Cudlitz as Dennis (Crossroads leader)
Lisa K. Wyatt as Pam (Kroehner mortician)
Lori Harmon as Chloe's Friend
Pat Destrocs as Chloe's Friend #2
Jules Tearle as Square Dancer
Jordan Brower as Topher
Uncredited as Chloe Yorkin

WHO'S THE STIFF?

Chloe Anne Bryant Yorkin, 1959-2001: On the day her divorce comes through, Chloe decides to celebrate by going for a ride in a stretch limo with her friends. Unfortunately she gets carried away and sticks her head through the open window, only for it to collide with an overhead traffic light and shatter her skull.

PLOT SUMMARY

It's a slow time at Fisher & Sons – there haven't been any new clients for a few days. Nate takes the chance to sunbathe in the garden whilst revising for his funeral directors' exam. David helps him revise, but it's clear that Nate needs to do a lot more work if he's going to pass. Later on, Nate approaches David with an idea for raising some extra funds in the short-term and marketing their services to a group of older people. He suggests that they rent out the slumber room for senior dance classes a couple of times a week, an idea that David loves.

Rico meanwhile is at Kroehner Services International – Matt Gilardi has offered him the chance to work on reconstructing the smashed-in face of Chloe Yorkin. Rico agrees to hire himself out on a freelance basis – $1500 for a one-off piece of work, as he has no intention of leaving the Fishers. Rico tells Gilardi that he will use his own materials as Kroehner's stuff isn't up to scratch. Of course, Rico ends up 'borrowing' the materials he needs to effect Chloe's reconstruction from Fisher & Sons' cupboards. Nate catches Rico in the Fisher & Sons prep room when he was supposed to be with Vanessa for her latest ultrasound scan, so his curiosity is naturally piqued. Nate notices that some material is missing, so he phones Vanessa to find out about her ultrasound. Vanessa unwittingly blows Rico's alibi, so Nate puts two and two together and realises that Rico must be moonlighting for some other company.

Claire meanwhile is starting her outward bound course. She makes friends with a young man called Topher who is finding the whole experience equally as miserable as she is. The so-called 'enlightenment' that Gary Deitman promised her has ended up as hiking, hiking and more hiking. Claire's mood goes from bad to worse when she discovers that her 'popular' classmate Parker McKenna is on the course too. Spotting a familiar face, Parker attaches herself to Claire and Topher, much to Claire's chagrin.

Ruth is enjoying eating lunch at work with Nikolai when Hiram turns up. He's cooked Ruth a special meal of jerk chicken – she's delighted and tucks in. Nikolai is very jealous of Ruth and Hiram's relationship and storms off. Meanwhile, David is watching the first of the senior square-dancing lessons when the young instructor Kurt grabs him and gets him involved in the lesson. David is instantly attracted to Kurt, and after the dance lesson is over finds himself accepting Kurt's invitation to go out on a date the next night.

Back at Kroehner's, Rico is working on Chloe when one of their other embalmers starts chatting to him. She lets slip that Kroehner was responsible for burning down the house on the other side of the road from Fisher & Sons – they did it as an insurance job and to cast a shadow over the small company with the police. Realising the depths to which Kroehner will sink in order to finish off Fisher & Sons, Rico is further amazed when Gilardi offers him a full-time job and the management of his own 'facility' within eight months. Gilardi gives him 48 hours to consider the offer.

One night on the outward bound course, Claire goes to try and find Parker. Hearing the noise of Parker having noisy sex from behind some bushes, Claire storms in, angry that Parker has 'stolen' Topher from her. However, Parker isn't having sex with Topher – it's actually Dennis, the Crossroads instructor and guide! Claire backs away, blushing with embarrassment.

Nate goes to visit Brenda and is shocked to see a broken pane of glass in her front door, which is wide open. Fearing that a burglar is still inside, Nate is shocked to discover a completely naked man wandering around inside Brenda's house. The man explains that his name is Connor – he's an old friend of Brenda's and he's been visiting for a few days. Nate suddenly realises that this is the reason why Brenda didn't want him to come over and visit. When Brenda gets home, Nate confronts her about Connor. She tells Nate that there is nothing going on between her and Connor – the reason she didn't tell him was because she knew he would get jealous and jump to conclusions... Trying to build bridges with Nate, she invites him to join her, Billy and Connor for dinner the next night. When Nate arrives home, he tells David about his suspicions over Rico's moonlighting. They don't know what to do. They are aware that losing Rico would be a terrible blow to the future prospects of Fisher & Sons, but they also know that they have no real hold over him either.

The next morning, Parker tells Claire that she hopes the embarrassment of the previous evening won't ruin their friendship. At first Claire is sceptical of Parker's overtures, but she soon realises that the school's 'popular' girl really wants to be her friend. Their bonding time together on the Crossroads Programme comes to an abrupt end, however, when course leader Dennis sends them home. His initial excuse is that Claire's map-reading was deliberately putting everyone's life in danger, but then he pulls out a bag of marijuana from her backpack. Dennis phones David and tells him to expect Claire home earlier than planned.

When Rico gets into work, David and Nate challenge him over his moonlighting. Rico tells them about the offer he's been made by Kroehner and says that he's seriously considering it. However, he allows the Fishers time to come up with a counter-offer.

At Nikolai's shop, Ruth daydreams about Hiram coming into the shop and passionately kissing her. Nikolai, working away next to Ruth, notices nothing. Meanwhile, Nate sits his funeral directors' exam. Even whilst taking the test Nate more or less knows that he's done so badly that he is certain to have failed it.

At Chloe Yorkin's viewing, Vanessa compliments her husband on his handiwork, describing the flawless reconstruction as Rico's 'Sistine Chapel'. She advises Rico that he should accept Kroehner's job offer, and Rico agrees that it's time to leave Fisher & Sons. That evening, David goes on a date with Kurt, 'the square-dance guy'. David is flattered by the attention of someone who is so much younger and better looking than he is, and unsurprisingly ends up in bed with Kurt shortly after.

Nate's evening doesn't go anywhere near as well. The dinner with Brenda, Billy and Connor begins with them all getting high on hits from a huge bong, and Nate has a very bad reaction to it. He begins to hallucinate that Brenda and Connor are kissing each other in front of him, and he loses his temper pretty spectacularly. Even though he's high, Nate realises that Connor has been sharing Brenda's bed, although once again she insists that nothing has happened between them. Brenda throws Nate out of her house, telling him to get some air.

Ruth, meanwhile, is watching a boring TV show with Hiram. Whilst he explains why the programme is so interesting, Ruth imagines Nikolai kissing her passionately, whilst dressed in traditional Russian Cossack clothes. Claire and Parker use the long drive back to Los Angeles to cement their friendship. Claire had always assumed that Parker was a goody-two-shoes, but is delighted to discover that she's actually a 'compulsive liar-danger-slut'! Likewise, Parker had always thought of Claire as a depressive goth chick, and is happy to find out that's not the case at all. Claire is shocked when Parker tells her that it was almost certainly Topher who told Dennis about the pot.

At work the next morning Rico tells the Fishers that he's decided to accept Kroehner's offer. Rico thanks the Fishers for their time together, but says it's time for him to move on. The Fishers are upset but wish him well. Later, Nate visits Brenda to apologise for his behaviour the previous evening. Brenda apologises too, acknowledging that she was scared of committing to her relationship with Nate and used both Billy and Connor as excuses to keep him at arm's length. Nate and Brenda make up, and they confirm that they both love each other, Nate even going so far as to say he wants to be with her 'long-term'. Just then David calls Nate with some good news – there's been a bus crash on a nearby motorway, and there are lots of locals amongst the fatalities: they will soon have some new clients following their long 'drought'!

Shortly after, Claire arrives home, exhausted by her overnight drive. David tells Claire that he won't tell Ruth about the pot that was discovered in her backpack. The two have an in-depth conversation during which Claire tells her brother that she knows he's gay. Claire asks what happened to Keith and says she's sorry when David explains that it didn't work out between them. They smile at each other as they finally acknowledge more about each other's lives.

THE PRODIGAL SON

Considering what a total and utter mess Nate makes of trying to patch up his relationship with Brenda, it's heart-warming to see their reunion at the end of the episode. Nate's jealousy rears its ugly head, and it's not a pleasant sight. In his defence, though, he is driven to such extremes of behaviour by Brenda's lack of communication and the way in which she pushes him away. When the two of them finally speak to each other properly at the end of the episode, their relationship really does reach a new level. They clearly commit properly to each other, something that they've not done so far. Things are looking really rosy for Nate and Brenda.

ANAL CONTROL FREAK

David takes the first step towards getting over his broken heart by plunging head-first into another relationship, with Kurt. This is a very different kind of David to the one that we're used to – someone who's been so wounded that he's willing to throw caution to the wind. Of course, David isn't making a rational decision here – he's not taking care so as not to hurt himself. The only person who we see get any insight into David's real character is Claire, with whom he has a touching conversation. David desperately wants to come out to everybody he cares about but he's still too scared that he could be rejected, so for now, it's still a case of 'softly, softly'.

MOMMY, DEAREST

For once in her life, Ruth has a choice to make between two potential suitors, and it's a choice that she finds tricky to make. She's still happy with Hiram, but seems to find him boring and predictable, whereas she's scared of the overly emotional and passionate Nikolai. The decision she makes will have repercussions on both her own life and that of her family.

TEENAGE KICKS

By going away on the Crossroads Programme, Claire does indeed find out a great deal about herself – but not necessarily in the way she might have predicted. Claire realises that despite her own insecurities, she has a great deal to offer in life to her friends and family. She stands up to the bullying programme leader Dennis and discovers that she's potential best friend material to one of the most popular and outgoing girls in the school. Most importantly, Claire realises she and her brother David have a lot in common. By instigating a conversation with David about his sexuality and lifestyle, Claire proves that she's mature enough to be trusted with important and personal information. Miss Fisher is certainly growing up.

DREAM ON, DREAMER

Whilst square-dancing with Kurt for the first time, David imagines one of the old men encouraging him to kiss the young instructor. When he does, all of the elderly dancers applaud wildly – in his dreams, of course!

Ruth has two visions, first of Hiram and then Nikolai kissing her whilst she is spending time with the other man. Nate has a vision of kissing as well – however, he pictures Brenda snogging the interloper Connor.

SOUNDTRACK

Gloria Gaynor – 'I Will Survive' (Chloe Yorkin's last limo ride)
T-Bone Walker – 'Strugglin' Blues' (Nate sunbathes whilst revising)
Caia – 'Whose Blues' (David and Kurt have dinner)
60 Channels – 'Ride With The Flow (Instrumental)' (Nate has dinner with Brenda, Billy and Connor)
Boozoo Bajou – 'Lava' (Nate talks to Connor)
Tulku – 'The Fire That Speaks' (Nate begins to hallucinate)
Ultra Naté – 'Twisted' (David and Kurt together)

SEX, DRUGS AND ROCK 'N' ROLL

Parker and Dennis enjoy an open-air knee-trembler, whilst David gets to show Kurt exactly how 'versatile' he really is. Nate's bong smoking nearly leads to disaster for him and Brenda (despite the fact that she, Connor and Billy indulge too), and the discovery of the pot that Claire had smoked with Topher leads to her getting booted off the Crossroads programme.

THE BRIGHT SIDE OF DEATH

Claire: So who do you think plays Parker in the movie of her life? Sandy Bullock or Julia Roberts?
Topher: Oh, please. She'd get one of those *Buffy* or *Dawson's Creek* chicks, tops!

Nate: That kid wants to jump your bones. Oh, come on, David. I watch *Will and Grace*. I've got gaydar.
David: OK, don't say 'gaydar.'

ISN'T THAT WHATSHISNAME?

Michael Cudlitz (Dennis) starred in the Steven Spielberg-produced TV mini-series *Band of Brothers* (2001) as Sergeant Denver 'Bull' Randleman. He was also a series regular in *Beverly Hills, 90210* for a year. He's also appeared in movies such as *The Negotiator* (F. Gary Gray, 1998) and the fantastic *Grosse Pointe Blank* (George Armitage, 1997). **Lisa K. Wyatt** (Pam) had a small role in *Legally Blonde* (Robert Luketic, 2001).

UNANSWERED QUESTIONS

✝ Will Parker prove to be a trustworthy friend for Claire?
✝ Will Ruth choose Hiram, Nikolai or some other option?
✝ Will David's new relationship with Kurt last?

EULOGY

Most *Six Feet Under* episode titles have multiple meanings, but 'Crossroads' really does take the biscuit. From the moment when poor Chloe Yorkin smashes her head into a set of traffic lights at a crossroads through to the Sierra Crossroads Programme, there are many obvious allusions. However, this title is even more relevant to the decisions that many of the characters face. Ruth literally is at a crossroads in her life – she has multiple possible routes ahead of her, and she's confused as to which one will prove to be the most suitable. Brenda and Nate's relationship also reaches a crisis point where they could as easily have split up as grow closer together. It's only really David who appears to be taking a wrong turning. Despite his momentary happiness, it's hard not to feel that Kurt really isn't the benign influence that he appears...

Two things strike as being unusual about this episode. Firstly, the victim Chloe Yorkin is not listed in the cast details – so we have no idea who plays the poor unfortunate! Secondly, the whole logic about who ratted on Claire about her marijuana stash seems really forced and nonsensical. In a show that prides itself on its internal logic and continuity, it's heartening to realise that something as petty as this is the closest you can ever get to a blunder or mistake in the production!

EPISODE 9
LIFE'S TOO SHORT

Directed by: Jeremy Podeswa
Written by: Christian Taylor

GUEST CAST
Ed Begley Jr as Hiram
Ed O'Ross as Nikolai
Eric Balfour as Gabe
Marina Black as Parker
Steven Pasquale as Kurt
Timm Sharp as Andy
Wendy Schaal as Vickie Dimas
Terrell Clayton as Eddie

Ted Marcoux as Sam Finelli
David Wells as Bland Funeral Director
Matt McCoy as Slick Funeral Director
Dale Raoul as Rosemary, Funeral Director
Jake Gridley as Anthony Finelli
Hal Ozsan as Man in Flower Shop
Louann Gideon as Grieving Woman
Gabriel Cade as Make-Out Guy

WHO'S THE STIFF?

Anthony Christopher Finelli, November 5, 1994-April 18, 2001: Anthony, six-year-old brother of Claire's former 'toe-job' boyfriend Gabe, discovers a gun under his mother's bed. Tragically for him and his family, the gun is loaded, and the boy accidentally blows his own head off.

PLOT SUMMARY

Nate has failed the funeral directors' licence test, and David takes great pleasure in telling him. As they score cheap points off each other, Gabe and Vickie, his mother, arrive to discuss Anthony's funeral. Vickie tells David and Nate that she wants a closed coffin, as she couldn't bear to see her son lying there. Considering the amount of reconstruction work that would be required, David is relieved. As the Dimases leave, Claire spots Gabe and rushes downstairs to find out what he's doing in her house. Discovering what has happened, Claire rushes after Gabe and tells him how sorry she is for his loss. He thanks her, and leaves to look after his mother.

Hiram reminds Ruth that the next day will be their two-year anniversary, so he offers to take her camping to celebrate. Ruth promises to ask Nikolai if she can take the time off. Although Nikolai is jealous that Ruth will be spending her free time with Hiram, he does eventually agree to let her take the time off. That night, Nate goes to see Brenda. He's overcome with sadness about Anthony Dimas's pointless death. Billy mocks him for getting upset, then shows his intellectual superiority by listing a catalogue of different cultural responses to the death of children. Brenda takes Nate's side and points out that (unlike 'widow' or 'orphan') there isn't even a word to describe a parent who has lost their child.

David copes with the stress of dealing with this unusually emotive case by going out clubbing with Kurt. Whilst dancing, Kurt gives David an ecstasy tablet – his first one. David has a night of drinking, dancing, kissing and sex, but feels the effect the next morning and has to leave the next intake meeting for Nate to supervise. Feeling rotten, David goes to the kitchen to get some aspirin. He suddenly remembers back to the previous night when Kurt gave him an extra couple of Es to hang on to 'for later'. David is staring at them in the palm of his hand when Ruth walks into the kitchen. Panicked, David pops the pills into the aspirin bottle and puts it back in the kitchen cabinet.

At school, Claire gets increasingly worried about Gabe. She asks Gabe's friend Andy how he's coping, but his lack of concern is astounding. Claire asks Parker what she should do, but her new friend advises her to steer well clear of a loser like Gabe Dimas. However, Claire doesn't follow Parker's advice and goes over to visit Gabe. He's not home, but his mother Vickie is sitting in the living room, almost in a catatonic state. Not knowing what to do, Claire goes home. Suffering from a stress headache, she goes to the kitchen and takes an aspirin. She bumps into Hiram and Ruth, who are packing for their camping expedition. Although Claire is quite disturbed by the thought of her mother going off into the wilderness to have sex, she tries not to show it.

Shortly after, Gabe shows up at Fisher & Sons. He's brought Anthony's football shirt along – he thought it would be a nice idea for his young brother to be buried in it. Gabe and Claire have a long chat about life and how they treated each other in the past. Gabe apologises for treating her badly, and he tells her about the horrible home life that he used to have; specifically, that his stepfather used to beat him up. Claire tells Gabe that if he ever needs anyone to speak to, he should call her.

Brenda decides to cheer Nate up by showing him how little he really needs to learn about being a proper funeral director. She's booked both of them to visit three rival funeral homes, to see how they go about dealing with their customers. Nate is aghast at this sick plan, but goes along with it out of a sense of horrified fascination and curiosity. The first home is a money-making factory where the only counselling that they are offered is 'matching caskets'. The second home tries to cheat them by overcharging for their services and offering substandard burial plots. At the third home, Brenda pretends to be a woman dying of cancer who has arrived to arrange her own funeral through a 'pre-need' arrangement. Nate thinks Brenda has gone too far and storms out. In the car, Brenda apologises to Nate, saying that she only did it to show him how he may have to deal with such a terrible eventuality should it ever arise. Nate forgives her. Later that night whilst lying in bed together, Nate tells Brenda why he was so upset by her performance earlier that day – he is truly terrified of the prospect of either of them dying. Brenda finally realises just how entrenched this fear is in Nate.

David, who is having great difficulty finishing his work on young Anthony, is delighted to get a call from Kurt. Needing to de-stress, David agrees to another night out. He goes to the kitchen to search for his ecstasy pills, but is horrified to discover that the aspirin bottle is missing. Claire sees David scrabbling through the cupboards and asks him what's going on. David confesses what he's looking for (and even admits that he's 'borrowed' Claire's black T-shirt for clubbing in!) and that he's panicking about his date with the 'square-dancing guy'. Claire tells him that she hasn't taken the pills, she doesn't know where they might be, and admits that she really likes this new David that she's seeing!

At the club, David apologises to Kurt for losing the Es and then makes a fool of himself by garbling a lot of embarrassing nonsense in front of Keith and his new boyfriend Eddie. Moving onto the dance floor, Kurt gives David some ketamine ('Special K'). Keith, who has observed his ex-boyfriend's illegal behaviour, leaves in disgust. Meanwhile, Kurt has found another man in the club. David stumbles across them kissing and is forced to make a major decision when Kurt suggests that they all go home for a threesome. David tells Kurt that at heart he's quite boring, and he apologises to Kurt for not being able to behave in the way Kurt would like. At that, David leaves.

In the woods, Hiram and Ruth enjoy a romantic dinner together. However, Ruth gets a headache and decides to take an aspirin. Of course, Ruth actually takes one of David's missing ecstasy tablets. Ruth dreams of following a bear through the woods and then running into her late husband Nathaniel. He tells her not to be guilty about her affair with Hiram – their marriage was effec-tively over long before he died. When Ruth wakes up the next morning, Hiram congratulates her on their lovemaking the previ-ous night – she's never been so passionate with him. Sadly, Ruth can't remember anything about it!

At Anthony's service, David apologises to Nate for being unpleasant to him over failing the funeral directors' test. David confides in his brother that he failed the exam on the first attempt too! The service is interrupted when Anthony's father Sam arrives. He attacks his stepson, blaming Gabe for not looking after Anthony properly. Nate pulls Sam away and takes him through into the next room, where he tells Sam that the death was a tragic accident. Claire takes Gabe away, trying to console the sobbing young man. Later that night, Ruth returns home. She's still smiling from ear to ear and tells David that he really should spend some time up in the woods because the sights, the sounds and the smells are just so intense. Realising that his mother is still probably a bit high on ecstasy, David decides not to tell her. Upstairs, Claire holds Gabe and strokes his hair as he cries his heart out on her bed.

THE PRODIGAL SON

In 'Life's Too Short' Brenda makes a concerted effort to try to understand her boyfriend's attitude towards death. She's aware that Nate is a living bundle of contradictions – he's a funeral director who is terrified of dying. When Brenda concocts her plan to help Nate simultaneously realise his own strengths and at the same time face his fear, she probably had little idea that he would react quite so strongly. Because Brenda simply isn't scared of death, it's hard for her to empathise with Nate. Eventually the two of them talk through the situation and hopefully a little bit of each other's perspective begins to rub off on the other.

ANAL CONTROL FREAK

David, under the influence of the far more experimental and rebellious Kurt, journeys still further down the road he chose in 'Crossroads'. This path is the one that David perhaps feels he *should* be following – a path that the young, confident and sexy gay men of Los Angeles all seem very happy with. However, this kind of behaviour just isn't David. It's not what he's happy with, and when he realises that he can't be part of a threesome, he (although high on yet another illegal drug) is still able to walk away. But David is still not ready to take responsibility for his actions – the fact that his mother ended up high on ecstasy because of his own stupidity should have shown him that his actions have consequences. He has not yet learned this lesson.

MOMMY, DEAREST

Well, who would have thought that Ruth would be the second member of the Fisher household to get high on E? Admittedly she is completely unaware that that's what's happened to her, but still the experience is an epiphany for Ruth. Whilst she's high, Ruth gets the forgiveness from Nathaniel that she's been longing for. She's now able to move forward with her life, thanks to the concept that 'Nathaniel' plants in her mind about Nikolai as a possible new partner for her. Drug-addled fantasy or genuine reawakening, 'Life's Too Short' marks the moment when Ruth finally shakes off the shackles of her former life. Oh, and in the dream we discover that Ruth was born on November 17, 1946, making her 55 years old and a Scorpio. In astrology, one of the primary characteristics of a typical Scorpio is their high sex drive. Perhaps this is an indicator as to how much effort it has been for Ruth to repress her natural sexuality. However, now that it's been unleashed…

TEENAGE KICKS

In this episode, Claire discovers a new role in life, as nursemaid for Gabe. Funnily enough, Claire adopts this role shortly after spending an evening bonding with Brenda over a joint. We know that Brenda (as *Charlotte: Light and Dark*) is one of Claire's juvenile role models, and we know that Claire looks up to Brenda as an intelligent, together woman. So is it surprising that Claire begins to mirror Brenda's co-dependent relationship with Billy? Claire ignores her new friend Parker's advice to leave Gabe alone, and instead she sacrifices her own needs to look after somebody else. Any one-way relationship is no relationship at all – something that Claire has yet to realise.

DREAM ON, DREAMER

Ruth briefly thinks she sees Nathaniel looking back at her in her bedroom mirror, but it's really only Hiram there. David gets flashbacks to his night partying on E and even imagines Ruth calling to him whilst having sex with Kurt.Ruth's ecstasy-induced dream sequence is especially fun. Ruth appears dressed in a kind of *Alice in Wonderland* outfit. She follows a giant bear (which wears Nathaniel's hat) and then ends up having a long-overdue conversation with her late husband. She even sees their joint gravestone in the place where the engine of the Fisher & Sons hearse should be.

SOUNDTRACK

TUU – 'All Of Our Ancestors' (Nate, Brenda and Billy have a tense meal)

H2S04 – 'Little Soul' (David arrives in the club)

Planet Perfecto – 'Bullet In The Gun (Solar Stone Remix)' (David dances, high on E)

H2S04 – 'I Need Feel' (David has a flashback to the previous night)

Vivaldi – 'The Four Seasons: Winter' (Nate and Brenda visit glossy funeral home)

The Januaries – 'The Girl's Insane (Thievery Corporation Remix)' (Kurt studies in his room)

Mandalay – 'Beautiful (Victor Calderone Remix)' (David and Kurt bump into Keith and Eddie)

Mellowtrax – 'In Da House' (David takes ketamine)

Liadov – 'The Musical Box' (Ruth's ecstasy-fuelled dream)

SEX, DRUGS AND ROCK 'N' ROLL

Gabe and Andy are too busy smoking dope to keep a proper eye on young Anthony – with tragic consequences. Both David and Kurt and then Ruth and Hiram enjoy nights of passion on ecstasy. Kurt gives David some ketamine (also known as 'Special K'). Ketamine is a tranquilliser used for surgical procedures on the very young or very old, and is a controlled substance in the UK and USA.

THE BRIGHT SIDE OF DEATH

David: Goddamn it, why doesn't anyone answer the door? Where is Mom?

Nate (smiling): OK, if you haven't slept with that guy yet, would you start? Cos I think it would do you a world of good.

Angry Man: Twelve dozen yellow roses, sent to this address, please.

Ruth: What would you like the card to say?

Angry Man: 'Fuck you, cunt!'

Ruth: I think it would be more personal if *you* write that.

ISN'T THAT WHATSHISNAME?

David Wells (Bland Funeral Director) recently joined the cast of the daytime soap *Days of Our Lives*, playing Carl Liszt. His oddest role to date must surely be playing the Cheese Man who haunted the characters of *Buffy the Vampire Slayer* in an episode called 'Restless'. **Matt McCoy** (Slick Funeral Director) hasn't let a couple of appearances in the later *Police Academy* movies hold him back. He starred opposite Rebecca De Mornay in *The Hand That Rocks the Cradle* (Curtis Hanson, 1992) and had a small role in the superb thriller *L.A. Confidential* (also Hanson, 1997) as the star of fictional TV series *Badge of Honor*, Brett Chase. **Terrell Clayton** (Eddie) has appeared in the TV show *C.S.I: Crime Scene Investigation*, and is sometimes credited as Paul Terrell Clayton.

UNANSWERED QUESTIONS

✞ Will Brenda ever be able to help Nate cope with his fear of death?

✞ Is Claire really the best person to be looking after Gabe?

EULOGY

As an episode, 'Life's Too Short' combines some of the funniest and some of the most heartbreaking sequences of the whole series. Although the death of Anthony's a really upsetting sequence, it's very important that *Six Feet Under* reinforces the fact that death isn't always something that can be laughed off. Had there been a comedy death every week (along the lines of Tommy Romano's encounter with the bread mixer and Chloe Yorkin's 'I'm the king of the world!') then the emotional impact of the whole series would have been lessened. The death of Gabe's brother is truly shocking. From the moment the death is signposted, viewers are holding their breath, hoping against hope that what they expect to happen doesn't. Sadly, this is not to be the case. Just as we flinch away from watching the death of a small child, so the impact of the death on all of the core characters forms the main gist of the story. It's their responses and reaction to the trauma that provides such funny incidents. For example, Ruth's trip to the forest is one of the most inspired moments of television in recent years...

EPISODE 10
THE NEW PERSON

Directed by: Kathy Bates
Written by: Bruce Eric Kaplan

GUEST CAST
Joanna Cassidy as Margaret Chenowith
Robert Foxworth as Bernard Chenowith
Ed O'Ross as Nikolai
Eric Balfour as Gabe Dimas
Wendy Schaal as Vickie Dimas
Timm Sharp as Andy

Illeana Douglas as Angela
Lene Woroboff as Lotte
Irina Maleeva as Irina
Lisa K. Wyatt as Kroehner Mortician
John Billingsley as Jonathan Hanley
Tate Taylor as Job Applicant #1
Scott Alan Smith as Job Applicant #2
Robert Richardson as Homeless Man

WHO'S THE STIFF?

Jonathan Arthur Hanley, 1946-2001: Jonathan Hanley, a remarkably tedious office worker who deals with customer complaints, drones on and on about his work. His wife Sally cannot take it any longer. Whilst cooking breakfast, she takes a frying pan and whacks him hard on the back of the head. She calmly sits down and eats his breakfast, finally at peace.

PLOT SUMMARY

David and Nate sit in the prep room, looking at the corpse of Mr Hanley. They joke bleakly that if he could be murdered for being boring, the same thing could happen to them. Nate then brings up the subject of finding a replacement for Rico. Although David is good at the enbalmings where the people died 'clean' deaths, he just isn't skilled enough at tasks such as complex facial reconstructions. David finally agrees, at which point Nate confesses that he has already placed an ad in the paper.

The brothers interview a number of weird, oddball and just plain unsuitable applicants for the job. The last interviewee is a charming, intelligent, dedicated woman called Angela. After she leaves, David tells Nate he should call her in a few hours, so they don't seem too desperate, before adding: 'Just find out if she can start tomorrow…'

That night is the launch party for Billy's latest photographic exhibition at a local art gallery. A swarm of people surround Billy, who politely excuses himself when he sees Brenda. She gushes about the exhibition, telling him that in her opinion it's his best work ever – 'very disturbing!' Nate then spots his mother Ruth, who has come to the exhibition with Nikolai. Brenda tells him that she invited Ruth as part of her 'on-going campaign to get her to like me'. Shortly after, a decidedly sozzled Margaret Chenowith staggers over to speak with her children. She drags Billy away from his sister, telling Brenda, 'You can't keep him to yourself all of the time.' Margaret tells Billy that his father won't be able to attend the launch party because he's busy helping one of his patients. Billy is upset that once again his father seems to make more time for his patients than for his family.

Ruth and Nikolai come over to talk to Nate and Brenda. Ruth tells them that Hiram is visiting his son in Portland, which is why she brought Nikolai to the party instead. Margaret rejoins the others, giving Nate a huge hug and a sloppy kiss, which shocks Ruth. Brenda introduces Ruth to Margaret, who drunkenly jokes, 'That explains why you're looking at me like I just took a giant dump on your front lawn.'

The evening then goes from bad to worse for Brenda when she spots Dr Gareth Feinberg, the author of (to quote Brenda) '*Charlotte: fucking Light and Dark*', whom Margaret had invited along. Margaret shamelessly flirts with Dr Feinberg, who congratulates Billy on his show. However, Billy is just as unhappy to see Dr Feinberg. To get away from him, Nate and Brenda walk over to the wall to admire the photographs. Suddenly, they come upon a huge, brightly-coloured photograph of Nate urinating against a brick wall. Nate is absolutely furious. A sympathetic Brenda asks Billy what he was thinking of. Billy tells them that he had merely seen Nate walking and followed him for a little while – the purpose of his art is to catch people off-guard. Nate doesn't believe Billy's explanation and storms out, followed by Brenda.

Later that night, Brenda fills Nate in on some background to Billy and his behaviour. When she was eighteen, she went on a trip to Europe. When her mother met her at the airport, she told Brenda that Billy had 'committed suicide' – either too drunk to know precisely what she was saying, or having a momentary Freudian slip. In fact, he'd been hospitalised. To prevent Billy from attempting suicide again, Brenda decided to give up her chance to go to study at Yale University, and instead stayed home to take classes at UCLA. Brenda promises Nate that Billy is only ever a threat to himself – he'd never harm somebody else.

Sunday morning at the Fishers' breakfast table and Nate tries to find out if any of his family are having a less complicated time with their social lives. David confesses he is no longer seeing 'the person' he was last dating, and Claire admits she is seeing someone, but decides not to mention whom. Later that day, Claire is hanging out with Gabe at his house. He is morose and she keeps trying to cheer him up. Finally, he has the idea that the two of them can pack some of Anthony's toys and give them to the young boy who lives next door. Just then, however, Gabe's mum Vickie walks in to find them packing away the toys, and snatches the box back. Claire decides to show Gabe something funny, so she takes him to the art gallery, to see the photo of Nate peeing. Gabe thanks her for cheering him up... and apologises for the way he treated her earlier in the year.

Later in the day, Gabe tells Claire that he has to take a long trip to Barstow tomorrow to ask his father for some money that he and Vickie desperately need. Claire agrees to go with him.

At first sight, new employee Angela seems to be everything the boys hoped for, albeit somebody with rather forthright attitudes and an occasionally less-than-dignified manner. Angela regales Nate with extremely intimate details of her personal life and sexual escapades. When she hears Nate have an argument with Brenda on the phone, she asks him some very personal questions about their relationship. Nate tells her to mind her own business, obviously uncomfortable at being around someone as open as Angela.

Meanwhile, Brenda confronts Billy about his recent behaviour and treatment of Nate. She begs him to stop and tells him that while she understands that it can be hard to deal with a new person in your life, Billy must. He promises that he will. She accuses him of 'fucking with my mind like Feinberg'.

At the volunteer food distribution programme, David momentarily fantasises about one of the homeless men propositioning him. Needing to get a breath of fresh air, he walks away from the table and runs into the now bottle-blonde Tracy, who is talking to somebody on her mobile phone. She is organising the food distribution volunteers for next week, and one of the new names on the list is his ex – Keith Charles. David finds out that Tracy has been asking around about him, and has discovered that he used to go to St Stephen's.

Dr Feinberg arrives at work to discover the door smashed in and the office vandalised, files scattered all over the floor and 'Nathaniel and Isabel' daubed over the wall. At the Chenowith mansion, Billy tears up the files on Brenda that he's stolen from Feinberg, and throws them into the swimming pool. Bernard and Margaret try to calm him down, but Billy yells a tirade of abuse at them.

David gets home and works on prepping bodies with Angela. She promptly begins to ask him about what men he likes to date, having cottoned onto the fact that he's both gay and obviously single. This is the final straw for David, who suggests to the rest of the family at dinner that night that they should fire her. Ruth tries to convince the boys that sometimes first impressions aren't always accurate (clearly describing her own feelings about Nikolai rather than offering advice about Angela). Claire tells her family that she has to stay overnight at the observatory tomorrow for astronomy class – a blatant lie that David and Nate play along with. Ruth agrees to let Claire stay out.

The next day, Bernard and Margaret invite Brenda over and try to convince her to convince Billy to check himself into a psychiatric hospital to undergo intensive therapy – possibly even including shock treatment. She tells them that they are insane, and leaves, angrily. She goes to see Billy and demands to know if he's OK. He reassures her that everything is fine – he was just having a bad day.

Angela has her lunch in the Fishers' kitchen with Ruth – after she spills some food on her latest body's wig and David banishes her from eating in the preparation room. Ruth initially seems quite taken by Angela, until the mortician starts to pry into her relationship with Hiram, at which point she clams up completely. David and Nate manage to completely turn Ruth against Angela when she discovers one of her precious glasses has been broken – they tell her it wasn't them so it must have been Angela who broke it!

Claire turns up at the high school gym for her meeting with Gabe. However, she gets a voicemail from him, telling her that he has decided to go to visit his dad by himself. Although Gabe thanks her for her kindness, Claire is still hurt and upset to be pushed away again.

That night, David turns up to help out at the homeless food distribution programme so that he can see Keith. The two begin talking and David helps him pack away the food. Tracy eyes them suspiciously. After they are done, the two get some food for themselves. They stop off at the closed art gallery and look in the window, amused by the picture of Nate. Keith asks David if he is still taking drugs, reminding him 'you know what that shit did to my sister...' David tells him that his whole episode with Kurt was a mistake, and he would never do anything like that again. Later, David takes Keith back to his apartment, attached to the Fisher house. David thinks they're there for a quickie, but Keith isn't interested in that, and walks away, bewildered at this change in his former boyfriend's behaviour. David later takes out his frustrations by dialling a phone sex line.

Ruth and Nikolai are thoroughly enjoying their date at a local Russian restaurant. Whilst Ruth is freshening up in the bathroom, she's approached by Lotte, a Russian woman who calls her a 'fucking bitch', convinced Ruth is trying to steal Nikolai away from her. Ruth puts her mind at ease – the two of them are just friends, eating dinner. She insists she would never threaten Lotte's relationship with Nikolai. The two hug, and Ruth leaves the bathroom and continues dancing and celebrating with Nikolai.

Nate finds Claire crying in the laundry room. She tells him everything that has happened, and how she thought Gabe really liked her. She doesn't understand why every time she feels 'really close to someone,' they 'just disappear'. Nate tells her that he thinks she's really talking about their father. Claire, wiping away the last tears, asks: 'Can't I just get upset without having to focus on what's really making me upset?'

After consoling his sister, Nate goes over to Brenda's house and apologises for overreacting about the photograph in the exhibition. He tells her that he wants her to need him. She smiles and tells him that she's trying her best.

The next morning, David comes down, hair unkempt and tie undone. Angela says, 'Rough night, stud?' Without another thought, David fires her and leaves. Angela begins to cry. She packs her things and leaves the house, weeping. On her way out, she tells Ruth that she has never before worked at a funeral home that was so sad, where so many secrets were hidden. She tells Ruth that she had tried to set David up with some guys, but she'd never met a gay man who was so closeted. She departs, leaving Ruth standing there stunned at this revelation about her son.

At Brenda's house, Margaret turns up to plead once again with Brenda to convince Billy to commit himself. Margaret finally tells Brenda the truth about what happened when she was eighteen: Billy never attempted suicide. Whilst trying to make a bomb, he set their house on fire. They also found notes containing the threats Billy made to the lives of his parents… and Brenda. Naturally, Brenda is furious. She realises that she has given up her entire life to look after a brother who has harboured violent thoughts towards her. Although she believes what Margaret is telling her, Brenda can't help but hate her for both keeping the secret and also for lying to her about Billy's true state of mind.

David calls Nate on his mobile to tell him the news about Angela. Nate decides to have a word with Rico to see if he can win their former employee back. Fortunately for the Fishers, Rico is indeed disillusioned with his new position. In the Kroehner preparation room, Rico tells Nate that Gilardi lied to him about both the hours he'd be expected to work and the pay he'd be receiving. Most damning of all, the work is unchallenging and dull and the prospects are not what he'd been led to expect. Rico agrees to come back to work for Fisher & Sons, provided they guarantee to let him have time off when his baby is born and more flexible working hours.

Claire gets increasingly worried about Gabe. She tries to call his mobile phone and it seems to be disconnected. His locker has been emptied out. Panicking, she drives over to Gabe's house and speaks to his mum, who tells Claire that Gabe never came home last night. Furthermore, there's no way that he could be visiting his father – his dad died when he was four. Gabe's final voicemail message to Claire reverberates through her mind: 'So that's, erm... that's it, I guess. Bye, Claire...'

THE PRODIGAL SON

The path of true love never runs smoothly – and in this episode, the particular pothole is called Billy. His jealousy towards Nate and Brenda's relationship is starting to get out of hand. Billy never adequately explains why he followed Nate to take the infamous photograph, and the stress of this public embarrassment for Nate combined with the shock for Brenda of seeing the detested Dr Feinberg leads to another big argument for the couple. However, on this occasion, it seems like the trouble and strife that the pair face is actually bringing them together rather than forcing them apart. Indeed, the more Billy tries to come between them, the stronger their relationship becomes.

ANAL CONTROL FREAK

Just as it looked as though a reunion between David and Keith was on the cards, David once again messes up his chance of happiness through his own stupidity. David misreads Keith's good intentions and hopes that he is in with the chance of sex. Keith pushes him away and storms off, no longer recognising his former boyfriend's behaviour. Desperate for some display of affection – or more likely, to regain some kind of control over his life – David goes online and contacts a man for phone sex. By now, the audience is practically screaming at David to get his act together and get back with Keith. However, it still seems that such a reunion is a long way off.

MOMMY, DEAREST

It seems that Ruth's drug-fuelled night of lust in the wilderness with Hiram has resulted in her questioning her relationship with him. Her newfound sexual freedom seems to have opened her up to exploring many other areas of her life – previously, somebody like Nikolai would never have stood a chance with the uptight Mrs Fisher. The dream sequence in 'Life's Too Short', where she and Nathaniel debate just what a sexual being she used to be, seems to be paying off here – indeed, Nathaniel did predict that Ruth and Nikolai would end up together… However, it's not just her own private life that Ruth reflects upon in 'The New Person' following Angela's little bombshell about David!

TEENAGE KICKS

The slow, gentle development of the romance between Gabe and Claire is particularly sweetly handled this week. Claire's maturity at allowing Gabe his own space, yet still being there for him following the tragic death of his little brother, is a sign of someone really thinking about another person's feelings before their own. This makes the double-whammy shock of the final few minutes of the episode so hard for Claire to take. Not only is Gabe still pushing her away (despite the progress in their relationship), but she finds out that he's repeatedly lied to her to make sure that distance is maintained. Once again, it's to Claire's credit that when he rejects her by voicemail, her thoughts aren't just for herself, but they're also for his wellbeing.

DREAM ON, DREAMER

All of the fantasy sequences in this episode belong to David, who's rapidly finding himself retreating into an imaginative dream world to escape the worries of his life. The first is a Bob Fosse-style song and dance number, with David getting back-up from a troupe of saucily clad male dancers. Later sequences feature David having two different types of fantasy with one of the homeless people from the food distribution programme – the first, a straightforward sex fantasy, the second a modern gay take on the stereotypical tragic ending to a Hollywood movie. As Keith bravely shoots the nasty man who has fatally stabbed David, the two doomed lovers are reunited. Keith begs David not to die just yet, telling him that he wants to make love to him one final time before he goes... This being David's dream, he is of course most keen to oblige Keith's request!

SOUNDTRACK

Andy Williams – 'Hawaiian Wedding Song' (Sally Hanley whacks her husband)

Michael Hall – 'Got A Lot Of Living To Do' from the musical *Bye Bye Birdie* (David breaks into song)

Uptight People – 'Get Uptight Man' and Candien – 'Ego Spiritual' (Billy's exhibition)

Astrud Gilberto – 'Aqua De Beber' (Margaret & Bernard talk to Brenda about institutionalising Billy)

Strauss – 'Acceleration Waltz Op. 234' (Ruth discovers the broken sherry glass)

Mahler – 'The Drinking Song' (David's dream about Keith shooting his attacker)

Troika – 'Murom' and 'Moscow's Golden Cupolas' (Ruth and Nikolai in the Russian restaurant)

SEX, DRUGS AND ROCK 'N' ROLL

Surprisingly, not much at all in this episode! Following Nate's bizarre, out-of-control trip in the previous episode, he vows to Brenda that he's never going to get high again… David's odd sexual fantasies keep things ticking over, but it's not until 'Jim' goes online and starts play-acting over the phone with another man that things start to get a bit steamy. 'Jim' plays the dominant partner, the 'top' – a direct contradiction to his previous claim that he's 'versatile'!

THE BRIGHT SIDE OF DEATH

Nate: Morning!
Claire: Morning. Pee on any walls lately?

Ruth to Lotte: Thank you! I've had the best time coming to this friendly restaurant and having you yell at me in the bathroom!

ISN'T THAT WHATSHERNAME?

Illeana Douglas (Angela) is a well-known face for movie buffs, having made a name for herself in many major hit films. Her resume includes appearances in *New York Stories* (for Woody Allen), *Goodfellas* and *Cape Fear* (for Martin Scorsese), *Alive*, *Quiz Show*, *To Die For*, *Stir of Echoes*, *The Next Best Thing*, a starring role in *Grace of My Heart* and (bizarrely) a film titled *The New Guy*… Spooky, huh?

UNANSWERED QUESTIONS

✝ What happened to Keith's sister with the drug problem?

✞ Does Nikolai still care for his on-off girlfriend Lotte, or are his feelings now all for Ruth?

✞ How much should we trust the word of Margaret and Bernard Chenowith?

✞ Has Tracy Montrose Blair figured out the relationship between David and Keith?

✞ Will Keith's new relationship with Eddie prevent him from reuniting with David?

EULOGY

OK, so if this episode is titled 'The New Person', who exactly is the new person? At first glance, it appears that it must be Fisher & Sons' new mortician, Angela. However, there are lots of other possible candidates: Nikolai is now the new man in Ruth's life; Ruth herself is almost a 'new person' following her ecstasy-fuelled reawakening; Gabe is back in Claire's life and could therefore be described as her new fella.

Poor Angela does get a very rough ride from the Fishers. She is remarkably accomplished at her job, never does anything malicious or negative, and seems to have a genuine passion and lust for life. Of course, this kind of behaviour directly conflicts with the most uptight and repressed family in California. Angela manages to alienate Nate, David and Ruth in rapid succession, simply by being herself, telling the truth and saying what's on her mind. In a house of secrets and lies, this kind of behaviour is simply unacceptable.

The ever-wonderful Illeana Douglas makes the potentially horrendous Angela into a very sympathetic (if somewhat blundering) character, and without doubt it's her scenes that prove to be the highlight of the episode, whether it's embarrassing Nate and David or blurting out long-held secrets to Ruth. There are plenty of plot revelations too, concerning Billy and his parents and the possible mental health of Gabe, but despite these dramatic shocks and surprises, this is a hilarious episode. One of the best of the season so far. Oh, and isn't it great to see Rico heading back to his rightful place with the Fishers?

EPISODE 11
THE TRIP

Directed by: Michael Engler
Written by: Rick Cleveland

GUEST CAST
Ed O'Ross as Nikolai
Eric Balfour as Gabe Dimas
Wendy Schaal as Vickie Dimas
Garrison Hershberger as Matthew Gilardi
Justina Machado as Vanessa Diaz
Joel Brooks as Robbie

Mary Gross as Floral Instructor
Michelle Ruben as Amber
Blake Adams as Brad
Patrick Cavanaugh as Mike Cooper, Dillon's Father
Veronica Lauren as Dillon's Mother
Jenette Goldstein as Obstetrician
Harry S. Murphy as Kroehner Funeral Director
Linda Klein as Delivery Room Doctor
David Ursin as Processing Officer
David Doty as Schraeger
Steve Hofvendahl as Dooley
Jonathan Brent as One-Night Stand

WHO'S THE STIFF?

Dillon Cooper, 2001-2001: A three-week-old baby boy, Dillon Cooper, dies suddenly in his sleep, a victim of Cot Death (known in the USA as SIDS or Sudden Infant Death Syndrome).

PLOT SUMMARY

David rapidly bundles a young man out of his bedroom, having picked him up online the night before. As he leaves, he catches the eye of Ruth, who is watering her plants in the garden. Still reeling from Angela's comments, Ruth sprays the young man with water from her hosepipe. A few moments later, David comes down from his apartment and exchanges pleasantries with his mother, unaware of her knowledge, her anger or her accuracy with a hosepipe.

Nate and Brenda are woken up by a phone call from Billy. Refusing to take the call, Brenda listens to his message as he rants and raves at her, calling her a 'goddamn bitch' for refusing to return his calls. Brenda is upset and is additionally troubled when Nate reminds her that he and David are going to be going to Las Vegas to attend the Annual Western States Funeral Directors' Conference. David is due to address the conference in Nathaniel's place, so it's something they can't miss. Promising not to think about Brenda whilst he's sleeping with showgirls, Nate heads off.

Nate explains to Rico that his first job on returning to work at Fisher & Sons will be to prepare baby Dillon Cooper. Although Rico tells Nate that it's not a problem, it's clear that the young man is deeply disturbed by the prospect of embalming such a young child – especially as his wife Vanessa is due to give birth in the next few days.

Whilst David is packing his clothes for the trip, Ruth tentatively tries to bring up a delicate topic of conversation with her son. Sensing what it is that she's about to ask, David quickly asks if it can wait until he gets back from Vegas. Ruth almost thankfully agrees to talk about it then. A few moments later, as David and Nate are packing their car, Brenda shows up, brightly telling the boys that she will be joining them on their trip to Sin City.

Claire is still worrying about the whereabouts of Gabe, so she phones Vickie Dimas again. She's horrified to hear that Gabe has taken an overdose of speed and heroin and she rushes to be by his hospital bedside. She finds Vickie and Gabe barely communicating and receives a mouthful of abuse from Gabe for bothering to show up. Hurt at his behaviour, Claire leaves him to his own devices.

Ruth gets a shock when she arrives for work. Nikolai tells her that there have been complaints about the quality of her flower arrangements. Nikolai's regular florist – the somewhat bitchy and camp Robbie – is delighted to see his 'rival' taken down a peg or two. Ruth is determined not to be pushed back onto working the cash till, so she decides to join a flower arranging class.

Rico and Vanessa have one of their final check-ups before the birth of their baby. The child seems to be fine, but the doctor is slightly concerned that Vanessa has mild pre-natal hypertension. This of course only adds to Rico's fears, particularly when he tries to begin work on embalming the Cooper baby and cannot bring himself to do it.

As the convention gets into full swing, David, Nate and Brenda bump into their old nemesis Matthew Gilardi. Nate wipes the smug grin off Gilardi's face when he gives the Kroehner man a pack of matches and some money for a can of lighter fluid, thereby telling him that they know about the burning down of the empty house opposite Fisher & Sons. That night, Brenda and Nate have a night on the town in Vegas whilst David goes back to his room to prepare his speech for the conference the next day. Unbeknownst to Brenda and Nate, an unkempt Billy has followed them to Vegas and is watching their every move.

The next morning, Gabe wakes up in his hospital room. He's pleased to see that Claire is still there – she spent the night sleeping in her car. This time, instead of pushing her away, Gabe tells her he's glad she's still around. Back at Fisher & Sons, Rico keeps breaking down when he tries to work on the baby's body. He takes a lunch break and goes home to check up on Vanessa. When he can't find his wife, he starts to panic, but she's just gone out to get some shopping. When Vanessa returns home, she comforts Rico and tells him that just because he's working on a dead baby, nothing bad will happen to their child. Rico returns to work and manages to complete the task of preparing baby Dillon's body. At the viewing, Dillon's parents thank Rico from the bottom of their hearts for making the goodbye to their son so dignified.

As Brenda plays the blackjack tables, Billy corners her, pretending that bumping into her in Vegas is nothing more than a coincidence. Brenda angrily tells Billy that she knows all about the bomb he tried to make when Brenda was about to leave for Yale and the lies about his 'suicide attempt'. She tells Billy that she wants nothing more to do with him and tries to walk away, but Billy grabs her and corners her. Nate arrives just in time and tells Billy to fuck off.

At the convention, David and Nate are angry to discover that Kroehner are using the reconstruction job that Rico did on Chloe Yorkin in their brochures as an example of the high quality of their work. David then delivers his speech on the future of the independent funeral home. When he notices Gilardi and many representatives from Kroehner in the audience, David throws away his pre-prepared notes and launches into a blistering attack on the big company's ethics and lack of real customer service. The Kroehner lackeys walk out of the speech in disgust, but David gets a rapturous standing ovation from the other small business owners in the room, and is hailed as the hero of the whole convention. David accepts an offer to join some of the other funeral directors for a few drinks, but Brenda and Nate decide to go out on their own and do some sightseeing.

David's new friends take him to a lap-dancing bar and buy him a dance from the voluptuous Amber. By now David is very drunk indeed, and when he leaves the bar he ends up calling a rent boy, intent on paying for sex with a young muscular hunk whose advert he's seen in a local magazine. When 'Brad' shows up, he looks considerably older than his advert! Still, David decides to take him to a nearby deserted parking lot and they have aggressive sex with David playing the role of dominant 'top'. Unfortunately, whilst David and Brad are mid-shag, a police car pulls up and they are both arrested for public indecency.

Back home in Los Angeles, Ruth's flower-arranging class starts off badly. The instructor points out that Ruth's arrangements are far too formal, too restricted, too 'tight', and suggests that breathing exercises might be in order to help her overcome her 'control freak' tendencies. Back home for lunch, Ruth sees Claire looking exhausted. Claire explains that she stayed out overnight in order to be close to Gabe, and tells her mother what happened. Ruth worries about her daughter's welfare and after taking some deep, slow breaths, calmly suggests to Claire that she should stay away from Gabe. Returning to her class, Ruth continues to breathe deeply and creates a stunning display of creative and relaxed flowers.

David is released from jail the next morning thanks to the intervention of Keith. David used his one phone call to contact his exboyfriend, and Keith pulled some strings to get the charges dropped. Keith warns David that he will never help him out in such a way again, and leaves David to cope with his shame and embarrassment alone. David returns to the hotel just as Brenda and Nate are getting ready for the drive back to Los Angeles. Still hungover and exhausted, David asks Nate to do the driving.

Ruth shows off her new flower-arranging skills to Nikolai. He's so impressed that he lets Ruth do all of the arranging for the rest of the day, much to the disgust of Robbie. Claire visits Gabe in hospital again. She kisses him and tells him that she loves him. He says that he loves her too. Vanessa gives birth to a healthy baby boy, named Augusto. Some time later, Brenda and Nate are looking at the photos they took during their trip to Las Vegas, laughing and remembering the fun times. They stop laughing when they see photographs of both of them lying in bed together, asleep. Neither of them could possibly have taken the pictures. 'Oh fuck!' exclaims Brenda. 'Billy…'

THE PRODIGAL SON

Nate and Brenda's relationship hits a turning point in 'The Trip'. Up until now, Brenda has always protected Billy from any criticism that Nate threw at him. She's always been Billy's protector. However, when Billy follows them to Las Vegas and continually tries to undermine their relationship, Brenda's primary allegiance shifts from her brother to her boyfriend. Although Brenda's not yet ready to take direct action against her brother, she *is* prepared to accept that Nate is in the right.

ANAL CONTROL FREAK

What a day of ups and downs for David – going from getting a standing ovation at the convention through to spending a night in jail. David's embarrassment at being outed to his new friends drives him to make a terrible error of judgement and phone up the rent boy. If David weren't so ashamed of being gay, he wouldn't have resorted to such risky and stupid behaviour with Brad. During the sexual act itself, David calls Brad a 'faggot' – it's not difficult to work out that David wishes that someone was punishing *him* for having homosexual feelings. Until David works through the guilt issues he has about his sexuality, he will never be happy. Thankfully, this episode does mark the darkest stage in David's journey to happiness.

MOMMY, DEAREST

A fantastic episode for Ruth lovers, 'The Trip' sees her finally accepting that she needs to change. Accepting that she's a control freak is almost akin to David accepting his sexuality – but Ruth is able to accept this aspect of her personality first. Learning to control her breathing and developing a new skill shows Ruth that she has a great deal to give, both to her family and to her suitors. Seeing her relax and come out of herself is a wonderful, affirming moment. It's also fantastic to see the gentle way in which Ruth tries to coax David into coming out to her. She doesn't want to actually have the conversation with him, so when David suggests they talk about it another time, Ruth breathes a huge sigh of relief – somewhat ironic for an episode that's all about Ruth learning to breathe properly!

TEENAGE KICKS

Just as Nate and Brenda reach a new understanding, so Gabe and Claire finally get round to saying that they love each other. Claire really does believe that she's in love with Gabe, but is Gabe actually in a position where he is able to genuinely love somebody? He's still an emotional mess, wracked with guilt for the death of his brother and trying to get over his overdose. Claire is determined that she will be responsible for bringing Gabe back from the brink by love and nursing. But isn't that exactly the same kind of smothering love that she hates her mother for? Surely nothing much has actually changed for Gabe. He still feels the guilt for the death of Anthony and will continue to do so, no matter how much Claire tries to make him forget it. By sublimating these negative emotions, Gabe is just deferring the time when he will have to face those feelings and deal with them.

DREAM ON, DREAMER

Upon seeing David's one-night stand, Ruth imagines David having sadomasochistic sex with him, with whips and chains.

SOUNDTRACK

Brahms – 'Lullaby' (Baby Dillon dies in his cot)
Dust to Dust – 'Submission' (Ruth's S&M fantasy)
Syd Dale – 'Everyone's A Winner' (Arrival at the Funeral Directors' Convention)
Tony Bennett – 'With Plenty Of Money And You' (Night-time in Vegas)
Syd Dale – 'Doo Wah Doo Wah' (David gets invited out on the town)
Chopin – 'Prelude #15, Op. 28' (Rico consoles baby Dillon's parents)
Francis Lemarque – 'A Paris' (Nate and Brenda have fun in the Paris Hotel)
Jungle Brothers – 'Sexy Body' (David gets a lap dance)
Afghan Whigs – 'Something Hot' (David calls the rent boy)

SEX, DRUGS AND ROCK 'N' ROLL

We see the after effects of Gabe's heroin and speed overdose and it's not a pretty sight, leaving him in hospital for several days. David gets to 'enjoy' a topless lap dance from the buxom Amber before deciding a bit of rough anonymous sex with a male prostitute is a better bet. Oh, and Nate and Brenda enjoy a night of passion in their Vegas hotel, little knowing that Billy's presence has actually turned it into a threesome...

THE BRIGHT SIDE OF DEATH

Brenda: I love Las Vegas! It has to be the most artificial place on earth!
Nate: Oh, you think so? More than Disneyland?
Brenda: Oh, come on! More than Japan!

Ruth: Do you think I'm a control freak?
Claire: Um... yeah. Where do you think David gets it from?
Ruth: Your father was very controlling.
Claire: Not like you.
Ruth: That's not nice!

ISN'T THAT WHATSHISNAME?

Veronica Lauren (Dillon's Mother) was a regular star of daytime soap *Days of Our Lives* and appeared in the 1991 revival of classic horror soap opera *Dark Shadows* as Sarah Collins. **Jenette Goldstein** (Obstetrician) was a former professional gymnast, and is probably best known for playing the butch marine Vasquez in *Aliens* (James Cameron, 1985). **Linda Klein** (Delivery Room Doctor) is also a professional medical examiner, having worked on countless TV and film productions.

UNANSWERED QUESTIONS

✟ Do Gabe and Claire really love each other?
✟ Will Robbie continue to hold a grudge against Ruth?
✟ How far is Billy prepared to go in order to split up Nate and Brenda?

EULOGY

In the grand scheme of the season's overall plotlines, 'The Trip' does feel like a bit of a filler episode, merely setting things up for the two-part finale coming up next. However, there is a great deal to admire, particularly in the development of the main characters. The artificiality of Sin City brings a lot of feelings to the surface, revealing the worst of David and Billy and the best of Nate and Brenda. Meanwhile, Claire continues her self-sacrifice campaign (a Fisher family trait – how's she going to manage to get that last nail in when she finally crucifies herself?) and Ruth's new personality continues to flower. All this, and the birth of a new member of the Diaz family. All together now – aaaaah!

EPISODE 12
A PRIVATE LIFE
(PART 1 OF 2)

Directed by: Rodrigo Garcia
Written by: Kate Robin

GUEST CAST
Eric Balfour as Gabe
Joel Brooks as Robbie
Justina Machado as Vanessa Diaz
David Norona as Gary Deitman (School Psychiatrist)
Terrell Clayton as Eddie
Brian Poth as Marc Foster

Arthur Taxier as Marcus Foster Sr
Joan McMurtrey as Patsy Foster
Zach Shaffer as Marc's Boyfriend
Eric Payne as Police Captain
Ted Garcia as TV Reporter
Jason Matthew Smith as Basher #1
Billy Rieck as Basher #2
Gunther Jensen as Fundamentalist #1
Stewart Skelton as Fundamentalist #2

WHO'S THE STIFF?

Marcus Foster Jr, 1978-2001: Beaten to death by a pair of homophobic thugs for showing affection to his boyfriend in public.

PLOT SUMMARY

Rico and Vanessa bring baby Augusto to see the Fishers. Ruth and Nate are transfixed by the baby, but David leaves quickly.

Nate and David face an uncomfortable intake meeting with the parents of recently murdered Marc Foster. Marc had never come out as gay to his parents, and they agonise over whether or not they were indirectly responsible. As David identifies with the case so clearly, he tells Rico that he will be handling the reconstruction of Marc Foster himself.

Gabe arrives for his first day back at school following his overdose. The other school kids are staring and laughing at him, and he starts to realise that he's now in the same boat as Claire – they're both going to be seen as freaks from now on. Brenda challenges her brother about the photographs he took of her and Nate in bed. He tries to laugh it off, but she is deadly serious – she tells Billy that she wants the key to her house back. He throws a childish tantrum, but Brenda's mind is made up and she throws him out of her house. Later that night, Brenda tells Nate what she's done. Nate's still concerned about Billy's behaviour and tries to get Brenda to take out a restraining order against her brother. However, this just makes Brenda even more infuriated that he's being insensitive about the difficult decision that she had to make, and the argument they have spirals out of control to the point where Brenda breaks off her relationship with Nate. She tells Nate not to bother giving her house keys back, because she had her locks changed anyway.

Meanwhile, Ruth and David are having dinner. Ruth tries to raise the subject of David's sexuality, heavily implying that she would love him no matter what. David pretends he has no idea what Ruth's talking about, still not ready to open up to his mother.

The next day, Claire has a meeting with Gary Deitman, the school psychiatrist. He's worried about her, and specifically concerned about the fact that she no longer takes part in any fun social activities. Claire explains that she doesn't want to be a 'normal' teenager, which is why she no longer sings, works on the literary magazine (which censored her stories) or the 'juvenile' debating team. Gary then asks Claire if she's dating anybody, to which she says no.

At work, Keith is told by his superior officer that he is to be a guard for the Marc Foster funeral, to protect the mourners from the inevitable anti-gay protesters. Keith is somewhat amused, suggesting that he has only been asked to protect this funeral because he himself is gay. In the prep room, David works on Marc's reconstruction, only to be taunted by a vision of the battered and beaten Marc, who tells David that they're both going to go to hell. David protests that God chose their sexuality so he must still love them –but Marc mocks and laughs at this statement, causing David further pain and angst.

At the flower shop, Ruth decides to have a chat with Robbie, hoping to ask him how he came out to his parents. Robbie (despite the fact that he is at times quite flagrantly 'gay') angrily retorts that not only is he offended by Ruth's assumptions of his sexuality, he also has no intention of sharing such personal information with someone he doesn't like. Desperate for some kind of insight, Ruth shares a deeply personal and embarrassing experience with him. She tells Robbie that when she first started dating Hiram, he asked her to masturbate so that he would know how to pleasure her. She was horrified by this request, because she had never learned how. So Ruth tells Robbie that she was taught how to masturbate by a hairdresser! Revealing such an intimate secret finally cracks Robbie's permanent sneer, and he and Ruth start to become friends. Robbie tells Ruth that he was never able to come out to his parents because he knew they wouldn't have been able to handle it.

On his way to collect a new body, Nate goes into a large, empty building. Quickly he realises that the phone call must have been a set-up. As Nate explores the warehouse, he sees photos attached to the wall, including one of Claire kissing Billy ('Your sister and me', reads the caption) and of Nate and Brenda together ('My sister and you'). Nate then enters a room lit by hundreds of candles. At the far end of the room is a body, covered in a white sheet and soaked with blood. Fearing the worst, that Billy has killed himself,

Nate kneels to examine the body. Billy jumps up and screams, terrifying Nate. Billy is highly amused by his latest 'exhibition' and grabs a Stanley knife, threatening Nate with it. Nate calmly tells Billy that Brenda dumped him, and quickly makes his excuses and leaves. Nate goes and tells Brenda what has happened, and although she's clearly concerned for him, she once again pushes Nate away, telling him to leave as she needs to sleep. That same night, David drives past the parking lot where Marc was beaten to death. There's a candlelight vigil taking place at the spot where the young man died, and as David drives past, he spots Keith's new boyfriend Eddie taking part in the mourning. Eddie briefly makes eye contact with David, which prompts the still-closeted young mortician to drive off.

Next day at school, Gary Deitman tells Claire that he saw her hanging out with Gabe Dimas, and wonders why she lied to him. Claire tells him that she was worried he would give her 'a lecture on inappropriate friends'. Claire asks Gary what she can do to stop Gabe from trying to commit suicide again. His advice is to make sure that she doesn't 'make yourself invisible' – however, Claire misses the point and tells him that she's not asking for help about herself. Later, Claire breaks down in tears in front of Gabe, telling him that she's worried that he will disappear on her. Gabe tells Claire that he thinks she's too good for him. Claire tells him that he's crazy, and they kiss.

David is still being taunted by the ghost of Marc, who appears battered and bruised, despite the amazing restoration job that David has done on the corpse. Rico enters the prep room and congratulates David on the best work he's ever done. Rico then starts to laugh about all of the 'homos' who have started to gather for the viewing upstairs, prompting David to finally come out to his employee. Rico is horrified and apparently disgusted by David's admission, telling him that back home in Puerto Rico, if men have those urges, they do it in secret and continue to behave like 'real' men. 'I am a man!' shouts David, but the mortician walks out of the conversation.

Later that night, Ruth asks Nate if his brother is gay. Nate refuses to tell her, suggesting that Ruth should ask that question to David herself. Lying at home in bed, Brenda hears the sound of breaking glass. She finds Billy in the darkened living room, shaking and covered in blood. He lifts his shirt to show his sister that he has literally sliced the 'Isabel' tattoo out of his flesh, telling Brenda that the only way to escape the nurse is to become different people. Now it's Brenda's turn – she must have the tattoo removed as well. A hysterical Brenda tries to escape her house, but Billy holds her down, ripping the nightdress off her back, preparing to carve the 'Nathaniel' tattoo off her back. In a last desperate attempt to break free, Brenda elbows Billy in the face. He flies back, hitting his head on the wall and falling unconscious. Brenda, shaking, calls for an ambulance.

The next day is Marc's funeral. As the police had predicted, such a high-profile death of a gay man has attracted a large group of homophobic protesters, many of whom are waving banners and chanting insults at Marc's parents and friends. David is so enraged by the comments that he rushes at one of the protestors and starts to beat him up, only getting dragged away by Keith. When they are out of earshot of the crowd, Keith starts to laugh at David – Keith told him that one day he would fight back against the homophobes, and that day has finally arrived. David apologises to his ex-boyfriend for his self-destructive behaviour, and tells him he wishes he could be as comfortable with his sexuality as Keith is.

Meanwhile, back at home, Claire has sneaked Gabe in, past the ever-watchful eyes of Ruth. They share a passionate shower together. Nate meets Brenda at the hospital, where she confides that she has finally had Billy committed to an institution for the mentally ill. She breaks down in tears, and Nate comforts her.

That night, David finally plucks up the courage to tell his mother that he's gay. Ruth asks him why he never told her before – he explains that he never felt comfortable, that he thought she would stop loving him. Ruth tells him that he is her son – her love for him is unconditional. Despite her protestations, David still seems unconvinced. As he gets ready for bed, David is still haunted by Marcus's ghost. David gets on his knees and prays to God to take his pain away.

THE PRODIGAL SON

Nate's love for Brenda shines through in this episode, where she has to face the toughest decision of her life – whether or not to have her brother committed. Nate does his best to protect Brenda, even when she pushes him away, refuses to believe what he's saying and finally dumps him. Ruth raises an interesting point at this stage – Nate has only ever been attracted to girls who made life difficult for him, getting bored with the easy-going, 'nice' girls. In the end, Nate is there for Brenda as she 'betrays' her brother, and it's that acceptance that makes the couple's very special relationship work.

ANAL CONTROL FREAK

When David strikes out at the Christian fundamentalist protester at Marc Foster's funeral, it's not hard to see what he is actually trying to do. This episode sees him finally realising that his long-held secret at home is blown – he acknowledges that well before he finally gets round to telling his mother. It also sees David coming out to Rico – his professional life. Even in his romantic life, although he isn't reunited with Keith, he has come to terms with who he is, gaining the pride and respect of his former partner. In fact, there's only one area of his life that David is still struggling with – his faith. The ghost of Marc Foster (a boy killed for showing affection to his boyfriend in public) taunts David with a succession of insults – for being gay, for being unable to come out, for the inevitable damnation to hell that his lifestyle will entail. By hitting out at the fundamentalist Christian protester, David is hitting out at the establishment of the church. He cannot reconcile his genuine love for God with the church's teaching that what he is doing is a sin. Until he can overcome this conflict, David will never be free of the ghost of Marc Foster.

MOMMY, DEAREST

Ruth's desperate attempt to understand her children and come to terms with who – and what – they are comes to a head in this episode. She's prepared to thoroughly embarrass herself in front of her workplace rival Robbie in order to help her son and to help understand what he might be going through. When she finally hears David's confession, it's clear that Ruth has learned a great deal about how she needs to behave. Instead of being a typical Fisher and repressing her feelings, she's starting to open up. Ruth's two conversations with Robbie are charming scenes, beautifully written and performed to perfection by Frances Conroy – one of the highlights of the whole first season.

TEENAGE KICKS

Claire tries desperately to keep her life with Gabe private. She lies to the school counsellor about the relationship, then sneaks him into the shower past her mother. However well intentioned she is, Claire is lucky the counsellor manages to get her to speak about her feelings. She's naturally scared about losing Gabe, and puts her own needs on the backburner. As the counsellor points out, Claire really needs to ensure that she doesn't become invisible – by subsuming her own needs into caring for Gabe, Claire is not getting what she needs from a relationship. In 'A Private Life', Lauren Ambrose puts in a particularly fine performance during Claire's second conversation with her counsellor, giving even more depth and subtlety to the confused teen, who is desperate to create and sustain her own private life.

DREAM ON, DREAMER

This week's only example of fantasy/dream sequences is possibly the most disturbing seen so far. David reflects his own personal neuroses and damage onto the recently deceased Marc, revealing a deeply troubled and split psyche. Logically, David knows that coming out, and coming to terms with his own sexuality, is the only way forward. However, Marc represents the guilt and repression that David has dealt with for 30 years, and the dreams of self-hatred and loathing prove that it's not going to be easy for David to get through this.

SOUNDTRACK

Buck-O-Nine – 'Who Are They' (The thugs pull up in their car)
Aquabassino – 'Nana's Waltz' (Brenda breaks up with Nate)
Peggy Lee – 'Everything's Moving Too Fast' (Ruth tries talking with Robbie)
Enrico Caruso – 'L'elisir D'Amore' (Nate goes to Billy's studio)

SEX, DRUGS AND ROCK 'N' ROLL

Again, not much in this episode – just Claire and Gabe's showery session.

THE BRIGHT SIDE OF DEATH

Ruth: How did you tell your parents you were…?
Robbie: 'Into flowers'? Well, it was obvious from the beginning. My first word was 'perennial'.

Protestor: God killed Marc Foster, and I'm here to celebrate.
(David punches the man hard in the stomach)
David: God just shoved your stomach into your lungs, and I'm here to celebrate!
(David punches him in the face)
David: Look, God just got you in the face!

ISN'T THAT WHATSHISNAME?

Arthur Taxier (Marcus Foster Sr) had a recurring role in the cop show *Hill Street Blues*. **Joan McMurtrey** (Patsy Foster) has been in *The Bold and the Beautiful* and classic private eye series *Simon & Simon*. **Eric Payne** (Police Captain) has appeared in, amongst others, the films *She's Gotta Have It* (1986), *School Daze* (1988) and *Malcolm X* (1992), all by Spike Lee. **Ted Garcia** (TV Reporter) is a real-life TV reporter for KTLA in San Diego.

UNANSWERED QUESTIONS

✝ Is David ever going to be totally comfortable with his sexuality?
✝ As Bernard and Margaret Chenowith are in South Africa, what are they going to say about Billy's sectioning?
✝ Is this just another example of Gabe leading Claire on? Does he *really* care for her at all?

EULOGY

Bringing together most of the themes explored during the past eleven episodes, 'A Private Life' seems to wrap up a lot of things: David has at last come out to Ruth, Billy is now in hospital getting treatment, and Nate and Claire are now in happy relationships. Well, actually, no. A stunning tour de force of acting, writing and direction, 'A Private Life' may actually be the heart of the season, but there's still a great deal more to come in the season finale.

A hint of the storm clouds brewing can be seen by the continued presence of Marc Foster. Previously, all the ghosts the characters have spoken to have disappeared by the closing credits – in 'A Private Life', Marc is still taunting David, testing his faith and his understanding and knowledge of himself. Just as Billy's madness is something that cannot go away without help, without facing the cause of the problem, so David needs to take a step further into his own psyche, to face his own demons, before he can be truly happy.

EPISODE 13
KNOCK, KNOCK

Directed by: Alan Ball
Written by: Alan Ball

GUEST CAST
Richard Jenkins as Nathaniel Fisher
Ed Begley Jr as Hiram
Ed O'Ross as Nikolai
Eric Balfour as Gabe
Justina Machado as Vanessa Diaz
Brian Poth as Marc Foster
Terrell Clayton as Eddie
Dina Waters as Tracy Montrose Blair
Tim Maculan as Father Jack
Marina Black as Parker
Timm Sharp as Andy
Garrison Hershberger as Gilardi
Frank Birney as Walter Kriegenthaler
Nancy Linehan Charles as Connie
Hayden Tank as Young Nate
Maximillian Orion Kesmodel as Young David

Giancarlo Rodriguez as Julio Diaz
Aaron Leigh as Dink
Cameron Watson as Doctor
Frank Crim as Convenience Store Clerk
Jamie McShane as Paramedic

WHO'S THE STIFF?

Lilian Grace Montrose, 1939-2001: Struck on the head by a badly aimed golf ball, Ms Montrose never knew what hit her. The ball was struck by Mitzi Dalton Huntley, the Southwest Regional Director for Kroehner Services, and Gilardi's boss.

PLOT SUMMARY

Nate arrives at Brenda's house. She's initially angry that he took a while to get there, but then he reminds her that he's been sitting his funeral directors' licensing exam. Brenda apologises, but asks Nate if he will go with her to see Billy in hospital. On the way, Brenda keeps blaming herself for what's happened to Billy, and wonders if it's her fault that he's turned out the way he has. When they arrive at the hospital, Brenda decides to go and see Billy on her own. She tries to apologise to him, but he won't allow her to – Billy takes full blame for everything that's happened, and tells Brenda he's sorry for trying to hurt her. Back on his medication, Billy cannot understand how he could possibly have tried to hurt the person who means the most to him in the whole world. On the journey back from the hospital, Brenda's guilt gets the better of her and she has a huge argument with Nate. For a moment, she takes her eyes off the road and the car she is driving is nearly involved in a head-on crash with a lorry. The car, out of control, shoots off the road and crashes.

David answers the front door to find Tracy there. He jumps to the natural conclusion that she's turned up to try and flirt with him again, but is embarrassed to discover that she's there to bury her Aunt Lilian. Tracy is in full professional work mode, and treats David in a quite patronising fashion, using the brutal negotiating skills she has developed in her career as a professional party planner. She breezes out of the house without signing the contract agreeing to pay for her aunt's burial, then spends most of the rest of the day faxing and phoning with yet more changes and demands for the funeral, driving Rico and David crazy.

At school, Parker invites Claire and Gabe to a party at her father's Bel Air mansion at the weekend. Somewhat reluctantly,

Claire agrees to go. Meanwhile, at the flower shop, Ruth gets a call from Hiram inviting her to dinner that night. Nikolai overhears the conversation, and jealously tells Ruth that she can't go as she has to work late. Ruth snarls back that Nikolai is abusing his authority and acting immaturely, which results in Nikolai firing her on the spot. Ruth goes home in tears and finds Claire asleep on the couch. She tells Claire what's happened, and Claire tells her mum that she's probably better off out of the situation.

At the hospital, Brenda finally wakes up from her crash-induced concussion. She has a bandaged head, and Nate has a few small cuts and abrasions on his head. Brenda apologises to Nate for almost killing them both, and promises that she'll take better care of herself in future. Nate tells her that he prayed – for the first time in years – whilst she was unconscious, and says that if she really does want to get married, he's ready to make that commitment. They share a kiss. Ruth goes for dinner with Hiram, who drops a bombshell on her – he's met somebody new, and suggests that they should split up. Ruth is just as surprised as Hiram when she says she's fine with the decision – their relationship obviously couldn't have meant much if she feels nothing about it ending.

At the next church council meeting, there is uproar owing to a fax that has been anonymously circulated, stating that 'Father Jack is Gay!' The church's most traditionalist deacon, Walter Kriegenthaler, protests that he was not responsible for the fax. Nevertheless, he still demands that Father Jack be fired for performing a ceremony of commitment for a lesbian couple – something strictly banned by church law. The deacons' meeting spirals out of control, and David is finally forced into a corner by Walter's cross-examination and admits that he's gay.

Later, whilst chatting with Father Jack, David is furious at the witch-hunt he's witnessed, and tells Jack that they should team up and fight the bigots. Jack, however, is not willing to stand up and be counted. He knows which fights he can win, and which he can't win – and this is one of the latter. To add insult to injury, he confides to David that he isn't actually gay, just that most people assume that he is! Finally, he asks David to resign his post as deacon. Dumbfounded, David imagines he sees the battered corpse of Marc Foster laughing at him.

The next day, Ruth gets a call from Hiram, begging her to come back to him, but she hangs up on him. Ruth catches Claire as she's on her way to Parker's party, and gets Claire to promise that Parker's mother will call her. The party is at a huge, sumptuous mansion. It's full of teenagers drinking, smoking pot, snorting cocaine and copping off with each other. Claire feels out of place but Gabe seems to be in his element. He gets chatting with his friends Andy and Dink, and after sharing a joint with them, they go out to get more beer. Clearly very high, Gabe pulls a gun on the cashier and demands money from the cash till, little knowing that all his actions are being recorded on CCTV. At the party, Claire falls asleep and dreams of her father. Nathaniel tells Claire how much he likes Gabe, but ominously predicts that Gabe will be joining him soon.

Nate gets some bad news at the hospital – during the routine CAT scan following the car crash, the doctors detected an abnormality. There's a growth on his brain that looks as though it may be AVM – arterial venous malformation, abnormally enlarged blood vessels that can cause seizures, loss of language skills, strokes or even death. Nate's doctor tells him that he needs to have additional tests, but not to worry too much – he could quite easily live for another 50 years with no major symptoms. Nate of course is left terrified by this news.

Later that day, David is having a coffee with Keith. David explains what happened with Father Jack, but is dismayed when he remembers that he has to deliver a sermon at mass on Sunday. Keith tells David that he's very proud of him, and is still more impressed when David tells him that he's finally come out to his mother. Back at Fisher & Sons, Nate is getting an earful of complaints from Tracy about the way in which she has been treated by David and Rico – that is, until Nate bellows at her, telling her to thank her lucky stars that she's healthy and happy, and that nothing else will be done on her aunt's funeral until she signs the contract. A shocked Tracy does what she's told.

On Sunday morning, on her way to church, Ruth stops at Nikolai's flower shop to pick up the rest of her things. She is surprised to find a drunk Nikolai there. She tells him that she's broken up with Hiram. Nikolai tells Ruth that she needs somebody who really loves her, someone who will treat her right and make her feel beautiful. The pair kiss and make love in the middle of the flower shop. Afterwards,

Ruth is vaguely scandalised to realise that she has missed mass. She tells Nikolai that although she will be his lover, she will never be his wife – she's already spent the first half of her life doing that, and she doesn't want to spend the last half doing the same thing.

Whilst Ruth is throwing caution to the wind, David is doing the same thing. Instead of delivering a straightforward reading at church, he takes the opportunity to deliver a monologue addressing the question of guilt. 'I've been ashamed my entire life. I grew up thinking I was unworthy in the eyes of God, instead of trusting God.' David finishes his speech, saying, 'How am I supposed to spread God's love throughout the world when I deny it to myself? God be with you all.' He leaves the pulpit, feeling very proud of himself, and glances up at a stained glass window. Although the image is of a man kneeling in prayer before Christ, it does look as though the image could be interpreted in a much more sexual way. After mass, several people come up to David and congratulate him on his speech – including Keith and Eddie. David is delighted that they came to witness his moment of glory. As Keith and Eddie leave, David sees the ghost of Marc Foster. This time, there are no scars and bruises from the gay-bashing on him – Marc smiles at David and thanks him, before disappearing.

Returning to Fisher & Sons in time for Lilian Montrose's viewing, David asks Nate to console a bewildered Tracy. When Tracy asks Nate why people have to die, he offers her the only words of comfort he can provide (to both himself and to Tracy) – to 'make life important... make each day matter.' That evening, Rico and Vanessa hold baby Augusto's christening party at the Fishers'. All of the Fisher family and their respective partners are there. Nate watches from outside the room, happy to see everyone having such fun. Brenda drags him back into the party.

Nathaniel Fisher Sr has been watching the party too. He smiles at the sight of his family's happiness, and turns and walks upstairs.

THE PRODIGAL SON

Just as Nate begins to think that he's overcome one threat (Billy) to his happy future with Brenda, the routine scan after his car accident leaves him reeling. The knowledge that he's suffering from a potentially fatal condition has a short-term positive effect on his relationship, bringing him much closer to Brenda. But yet again Nate behaves like a typical Fisher and decides not to tell her what's happening. By resorting to yet more subterfuge and deceit, Nate puts his relationship at long-term risk.

ANAL CONTROL FREAK

David's journey through to self-belief and understanding about himself comes to its natural conclusion in this episode. After coming out to his family and his mother, he now finds the strength to come out to his church. It's quite a traumatic experience because this is the only time he's directly rejected for his sexuality. It is that very act of accepting that not everyone will continue to love him for telling the truth that makes David a stronger person. Indeed, it's this strength and this insight that enables David to shake off Marc Foster's ghost that had been haunting him for so long. Even though he's not reunited with his true love Keith, David is now able to take his first steps as a much happier human being.

MOMMY, DEAREST

Ruth shocks herself – and us! – by making passionate love on the floor of the flower shop with Nikolai. Ruth's choices are not predictable. Instead of staying with the cultured, intelligent, middle-class Hiram, she's almost delighted when he dumps her. She chooses to be with the passionate, common, barely literate Nikolai, and it's the making of her. She's learnt how to breathe, how to accept that things in life change, and she's even learnt how to enjoy sex. However, she knows what she's not prepared to do, and firmly tells Nikolai that she will never marry him. Yes, Ruth has indeed come on in leaps and bounds – but surely the years of ingrained behaviour patterns that she has lived by can't just get rewritten so quickly?

TEENAGE KICKS

Claire gets a worrying portent from her 'father' in this episode about the commitment she has made to Gabe. When Nathaniel tells her that Gabe will be in his 'neck of the woods' soon, Claire gets a bit of a wake-up call. Although she feels protective towards Gabe, she knows that his behaviour will cause her heartache. However at this point in time, Claire's not prepared to face that worry.

DREAM ON, DREAMER

Nate gets a visitation by his father, mocking him about his new mortality. Claire also dreams of her father several times, most significantly when he predicts that her boyfriend Gabe will soon be 'joining him'.

David continues to be haunted by Marc Foster's bruised and battered ghost, until the moment when he exorcises his own guilt about being gay and Christian. He also briefly imagines the whole church congregation wildly applauding his brave statement, but this is sadly just a figment of his own imagination.

Brenda, whilst concussed and sedated, has a particularly vivid dream of flying with dolphins. She tells Nate that in the dream Drew Barrymore was her best friend and that a Versace-dressed shark, played by Courtney Love, was chasing them. Bonkers!

SOUNDTRACK

Eleni Mandel – 'Pauline' (Brenda asks Nate to come with her to visit Billy)

King Cobb Steelie – 'Mayday' (Claire and Gabe arrive at Parker's party)

Ettenne De Crecy – 'Scratched' (Gabe's friends talk about doing a 'beer cow')

Beta Band – 'Squares' (Claire walks in on Parker and Warren)

Cher – 'Gypsies, Tramps And Thieves' (Gabe robs the convenience store)

Black Rebel Motorcycle Club – 'Red Eyes And Tears' (Claire talks to
    Nathaniel's ghost)
Frederic Chopin – 'Prelude Op. #28' (Lilian Montrose's viewing)
Cachaito – 'Mis Dos Pequenas' (Baby Augusto's christening)

SEX, DRUGS AND ROCK 'N' ROLL

Ruth and Nikolai's (thankfully) off-screen coupling in the flower
shop is a bit of a shock. Parker's party is a bit of a pharmacological
pick 'n' mix, with people doped up (most notably Gabe and his
friends) and snorting cocaine all over the place.

THE BRIGHT SIDE OF DEATH

Hiram: I thought you'd be more upset.
Ruth: Hiram, please, go, explore. You owe it to yourself and
    whoever she is. Maybe the two of you could have something, as
    you say, 'profound.' Lord knows we don't. If it was, this would
    be a lot more difficult, wouldn't it?
Hiram: Well, it is difficult – for me.
Ruth: Let's order dessert. That'll cheer you up.

Nate (laughs, then gets serious): When you were unconscious, I
    prayed. You know how long it's been since I prayed? I have
    never prayed like this!
Brenda: Because of me you've become... born again! I'm so sorry.

UNANSWERED QUESTIONS

✝ Will Nate's condition really prove life-threatening?
✝ Are Ruth and Hiram really over? And is Nikolai really the man
    for her?
✝ Is Gabe on his way to join Nathaniel? And just how long will it
    take for the police to track him down from the CCTV footage?
✝ Will Brenda ever get over the guilt of committing her brother?

✝ And just who exactly was dreaming about seeing Nathaniel Fisher in the final moments of the episode? Or were we, as the audience, privy to seeing an actual ghost?

EULOGY

Yet another astonishing episode, 'Knock, Knock' finishes off the first season of *Six Feet Under* on an amazing high note. We've been following David's journey towards happiness throughout the whole of the season, and it's a joy to see him finally at peace with himself and God. It's also fantastic to see Ruth with a man who may actually make her truly happy. However, there are ominous signs for the future of these characters. Nate's illness casts a shadow over his future happiness with Brenda, just as Nathaniel's words of caution could spell tragedy for Claire. However, the overall feeling is that we've just had as close as we're ever likely to get to a traditional 'happy ending', and after the year of tragedy and sadness that the Fishers have suffered, we're keen to enjoy that upbeat conclusion with them.

SEASON
TWO

EPISODE 14
IN THE GAME

Directed by: Rodrigo Garcia
Written by: Alan Ball

GUEST CAST

Richard Jenkins as Nathaniel Fisher
Ed O'Ross as Nikolai
Eric Balfour as Gabe
Terrell Clayton as Eddie
Mary-Pat Green as Priest

Shawn Hatosy as Brody Farrell
Alexandra Holden as Becky Maxwell (Rebecca Leah Milford)
Geoffrey Nauffts as AVM Specialist (Dr Di Paulo)
Barbara Tarbuck as STD Clinic Doctor
Melissa Marsala as Angelica
Denalda Williams as Becky's Manager
Scott Atkinson as Kevin Miller
Cleo King as Life
Stanley Kamel as Death
David Shatraw as Shiatsu Client
Ben Scott as Butcher

WHO'S THE STIFF?

Rebecca Leah Milford, 1980-2001: Collapsed and died in a toilet after taking an overdose of cocaine.

PLOT SUMMARY

Nate and Brenda make love, but it's 'not going to happen' for Brenda on this occasion. She's not happy with her life following the car crash – it's as if she's living somebody else's life. Nate thinks that she might be depressed.

At Fisher & Sons, Rico introduces David to his sister-in-law Angelica, who's currently starring in a horror film. One of her co-stars was the late Rebecca Milford, and the rest of the cast are paying for her funeral as she has no other family. During the induction, David gets a call from Kevin Miller, a fireman whose personal ad he responded to. They decide to meet for coffee. Rico tries to find the best way for Rebecca to be remembered, but her cheapskate (and rather stupid) co-stars don't help much.

Gabe and Claire are at the beach, enjoying the summer weather. She asks him why he wasn't at school – he tells her that he went to the car museum with Andy. She's worried about him, and he apologises, telling her that she doesn't need to fear for him as long as they're together.

Whilst Nate undergoes another MRI scan, David gets mostly good news from his STD clinic – his unsafe encounter in Las Vegas has resulted in him picking up gonorrhea, but thankfully nothing more serious. Ruth and Claire have a conversation about how they feel about David's sexuality – mostly because of the *Now That You Know* book Ruth's reading. David's date seems to go really well until all of a sudden Kevin Miller calls it a day, claiming that he doesn't 'feel much of a spark'.

Nate's meeting with specialist Dr Di Paulo shows that his condition is almost certainly AVM. He gives Nate three options – cranial surgery, embolisation or radiation therapy, none of which sound like either a sensible or comforting solution. Following the meeting, Nathaniel appears in the car with Nate – actually driving the car in Nate's mind – and laughs at him about his condition and the fact that he could drop dead despite his healthy lifestyle.

Over dinner, Ruth breaks the news that she's in 'a sexual relationship' with Nikolai. She invites Brenda, Gabe and any 'special friend' of David's over for a meal. That night, Rico asks a favour of Nate – to drop Rebecca Milford off at the crematorium because he's really busy and Vanessa is run ragged with the children. Nate says he's sorry, but he can't.

David goes to Sunday church at St Stephen's. After the service, he has breakfast with Keith and Eddie. They seem to be very happy together, much to David's dismay. Everyone begins to arrive for the big family Sunday dinner. Claire shows Gabe around the prep room, and Nate takes an aspirin from the kitchen cupboard for another headache. The small talk before the meal becomes increasingly awkward, and Nikolai's somewhat excessive grace raises a few smiles until Nate's strange behaviour starts to attract everyone's attention. Brenda suddenly realises what's wrong with her boyfriend – he's as high as a kite. He's accidentally taken the second ecstasy pill that David hid in the aspirin bottle months before. After dinner, Brenda decides to leave Nate for his brother (who was responsible for him getting in that situation) to look after, telling him to call her next week after he's crashed.

Nate falls asleep on the sofa, watching television. He has a particularly vivid dream of his father playing Chinese Checkers for money with 'Life' and 'Death', who invite him to join in the game – 'You're either in the game or out of it,' says Death. 'On or off the bus, if you prefer,' adds Nathaniel. As Death and Life engage in a spot of spontaneous coupling, Nathaniel strokes his son's head.

David calls Keith to thank him for their continuing friendship, but when Keith shows no empathy towards the troubled feelings his ex still has for him, David hangs up. Ruth meets David in the kitchen, where she apologises for arranging the whole ghastly dinner, and asks if Nate now has a problem with drugs.

It's Rebecca Milford's memorial service. David confesses to Nate that it might have been his fault for putting the ecstasy in the aspirin bottle. Instead of shouting at his brother, Nate asks if he can possibly get some more. Rebecca's co-star and 'kind of ex' Brody sings a diabolically naff and inappropriate eulogy for her. Rico's sister-in-law Angelica argues with him about the money they are meant to be paying for Rebecca's funeral, but then she stuns him by saying that Vanessa just borrowed $500 to pay for baby Augusto's nappies. Claire is horrified when she stumbles across Brody and his co-stars snorting cocaine mixed with Rebecca's ashes – she gives them a tongue-lashing but Nate tells her to back off.

Later, David calls Nate whilst he's at the beach with Brenda. Nate's just passed his funeral directors' exam, and David tells him how proud he is. Nate asks if he can go over to Brenda's house later on, but she asks if she can be on her own, claiming to be 'fucked up' but that she can fix it.

Staring out to the ocean on his own, Nate pictures himself walking headlong into the sea. Then suddenly he's back on the shore, with Nathaniel sitting next to him. 'You're in the game now, buddy boy. Whether you like it or not,' his father quips enigmatically.

THE PRODIGAL SON

Nate begins the uncomfortable and scary process of coming to terms with his AVM in this episode. His visit to the doctor seems to offer very little support or comfort, so what does he do? He keeps the news of the condition to himself. Showing behaviour patterns consistently typical of the Fisher family, Nate decides that it's better not to burden the rest of his family or his girlfriend with his news. Looking at Brenda's slightly odd behaviour, perhaps this is understandable, but why is she so depressed?

ANAL CONTROL FREAK

David seems a lot happier at the start of the second season. Following the trauma of coming out, he is more at peace with himself, but still very aware that he's on his own. He decides to get back in the dating game, but when things go awry there's only one person he still thinks about – Keith. At the moment, Keith seems far too happy with his new beau Eddie to even give David a second thought – but will the situation stay that way?

TEENAGE KICKS

Following her father's warning at the end of the last series, Claire is beginning to slowly wake up to Gabe's character flaws. She's finally starting to understand that going out with someone so unstable can only have a negative effect on her life. Having seen the impact that hard drugs can have on people, it's not surprising just how strongly Claire reacts to seeing Brody and his fellow actors snorting a mix of cocaine and Rebecca's ashes.

DREAM ON, DREAMER

Nate imagines strangling his insincere AVM specialist. Shortly afterwards, Nathaniel appears in Nate's car and takes the mickey out of Nate for his 'healthy' lifestyle. After seeing Eddie and Keith so happy together, David imagines himself stark naked in the middle of the *Mr Gay Black American* show.

Nate's ecstasy-fuelled dream about 'Life' and 'Death' is particularly bizarre.

SOUNDTRACK

Lamb – 'Heaven'/Stereo MCs – 'Deep Down And Dirty'/Aquanot – 'True Love (Petalpusher remix)'/MJ Cole – 'Sincere (Petalpusher Remix)' (Becky's final few hours of life)

Lux – 'Northern Lights' (David meets his date Kevin)

Peggy Lee – 'I Love Being Here With You' (Nate drives in the car with Nathaniel)

PJ Harvey – 'One Time Too Many' (Brenda cleans out her wardrobe and smokes a joint)

H.A.L.O. – 'Eclipsed (LFO remix)' (Brenda massages an arrogant client)

Albinoni – 'Violin Concerto In F Major, Op. 9, No. 10' (Waiting for dinner)

Beethoven – 'Opus 18, No. 6' (Nate gets high)

SEX, DRUGS AND ROCK 'N' ROLL

Rebecca Milford dies in a snowstorm of epic proportions, so it's fitting (in an exceptionally perverse way) that her 'friends' continue to celebrate her life by snorting her up their own noses. Nate's trip on ecstasy is something he enjoys so much that he asks his brother to try and get him some more pills!

THE BRIGHT SIDE OF DEATH

Ruth: Have you ever had any feelings of same-sex attraction…? It's nothing to be ashamed of. When I was your age, I actually had a little crush on Jane Fonda.
Claire: Well, she's single again, so now's your chance.

Ruth: One of my sons is high on drugs. What should I do? Intervene? Join a support group?

ISN'T THAT WHATSHISNAME?

Shawn Hatosy (Brody Farrell) has appeared in the movies *The Postman* (Kevin Costner, 1997), *The Faculty* (Robert Rodriguez, 1998) and *John Q* (Nick Cassavetes, 2000). **Mary-Pat Green** (Priest) was a regular in the American series *Any Day Now*, playing Odessa from 1998-2000. **Alexandra Holden** (Becky Maxwell) was Bruce Willis's daughter Elizabeth (and Ross's girlfriend) in the sixth series of the sitcom *Friends* and played Jane Wilco in the legal comedy drama *Ally McBeal*. **Geoffrey Nauffts** (AVM Specialist) appeared in the US series *The Commish*. In no way typecast, **Barbara Tarbuck** (STD Clinic Doctor) played a doctor in the long-running glam-soap *Falcon Crest*, a nurse on *Santa Barbara* and was a regular on *General Hospital*. The awesome **Cleo King** (Life) is a familiar face on American commercials. Her film credits include *Six Degrees of Separation* (Fred Schepisi, 1993) *Magnolia* (Paul Thomas Anderson, 1999) and *Dude, Where's My Car?* (Danny Leiner, 2000). **Stanley Kamel** (Death) was a regular on the daytime soap *Days of Our Lives*, appeared in *Beverly Hills, 90210* (as Tony Marchette) and guest starred in *Murder One* (as Dr Graham Lester).

UNANSWERED QUESTIONS

✟ What is the matter with Brenda? Why is she so depressed?
✟ Will Nate ever get the courage to tell his family about the AVM?

EULOGY

Following the painful and angst-ridden final few episodes of Season One, 'In the Game' comes as something of a breath of fresh air. There's a lot of bleakness, yes, but there are so many funny and slightly perverse moments that you almost forget the nastiness. Just as the audience tries to come to terms with the potential death sentence looming over Nate, we get to see him high as a kite having a hilarious hallucination about life and death. Only in a programme as clever as *Six Feet Under* can you have the punchline to a joke delivered weeks and weeks after you think it's already been said – didn't we all think that Ruth had taken *both* pills while she was off camping with Hiram? Genius!

EPISODE 15
OUT, OUT, BRIEF CANDLE

Directed by: Kathy Bates
Written by: Laurence Andries

GUEST CAST
Justina Machado as Vanessa Diaz
Julie White as Mitzi Dalton Huntley
Timm Sharp as Andy
Alice Krige as Alma
Joel Brooks as Robbie
Garrison Hershberger as Gilardi
Marina Black as Parker
Nicki Micheaux as Karla
Aysia Polk as Taylor
Ricardo Antonio Chavira as Ramon
Aaron Leigh as Dink

Page Kennedy as Josh Langmead
Tuc Watkins as Trevor
Judith Hoag as Dawn
Eddie Jemison as Casket Salesman
Shashawnee Hall as Richard Langmead
Dee Freeman as Susan Langmead
Julianna McCarthy as Beatrice
Katie Mitchell as Sheila
Susan Merson as Realtor

Evan Arnold as Graduate
Grant Thompson as Sam
Brian Tahash as Coach
Drake Johnston as Will

WHO'S THE STIFF?

Joshua Peter Langmead, 1981-2001: A perfectly fit and healthy young man, Joshua collapses and dies after training for football.

PLOT SUMMARY

Brenda is putting the final arrangements to a dinner menu. She's expecting her first ever boyfriend, Trevor, and his wife and son to come over, and wants Nate's advice about what to serve him.

Mitzi Dalton Huntley arrives at Kroehner, gunning for blood. Because of Matt Gilardi's inability to sign up Fisher & Sons, she fires him on the spot.

Josh Langmead's parents bring his American football shirt to the induction meeting, intending for their son to be buried in it. The Langmeads decide to opt for the expensive Titan 4 coffin for their son: 'It's only money,' they say. Nate is freaked out because this young healthy man suddenly collapsed and died from a brain condition. He keeps seeing Josh Langmead's 'ghost' crying about his sudden death. Just then Nate gets a phone call telling him that the Titan coffin has been discontinued and the replacement is yet more expensive.

Rico and Vanessa are looking for a new home. Rico takes his cousin Ramon along to see the house they like because he's a handyman and builder. Ramon says it's mostly OK, and Rico and Vanessa decide to try and put an offer in for it. Rico asks David and Nate for a loan of $11,000 to make the full 20 per cent deposit on the house. David says he'll think about it, and tells Rico he'll have a decision by tomorrow.

Gabe is concerned about the fact that the CCTV footage of the robbery is now being circulated throughout schools. His friends Dink and Andy aren't coping either. Andy has a bizarre fit of some sort in front of Claire and then collapses.

At work, Ruth is somewhat taken aback when Robbie tells her that he 'forgives' her for supplanting him at Nikolai's shop, for destroying 'the natural order of the universe, cupcake!' She initially resents this but then Robbie tells Ruth about the self-improvement course he's been attending, called 'The Plan'. It's a multi-discipline course that enables its students to rebuild their lives plank by plank and get what they want. Robbie asks Ruth to come to his graduation ceremony, and she reluctantly agrees.

Nate and David go to visit a coffin showroom, a 'completely interactive retail experience' that David describes as 'fucking gorgeous'. 'I have seen the future and this is it!' says the enthused younger brother. They decide to buy a coffin display wall for $20,000 including installation and a repainting job.

The next day, Mitzi arrives at Fisher & Sons. When the brothers discover that Mitzi is from Kroehner, their initial polite behaviour turns sour, with Nate in particular being extremely rude to her. She tells them that she's fired Matt and that, as a gesture, she wants to do 'a little damage control'. When Nate tells her to shove her gesture up her ass, she leaves.

Later that day, Nate has a word with Rico. Because of the investment in the coffin wall, they are not going to be able to loan him the money. Rico is angry but Nate points out that he's not family – he's an employee, and he can't expect to be treated any better than he already is. Nate feels very guilty about the decision. Later, as Nate is working in the prep room, Josh speaks to him about how scared he is. Nate angrily retorts that 'everybody dies – what makes you so fucking special?'

At Robbie's graduation ceremony, the motivational speaker Alma and the suffering and strength of the graduates transfix Ruth.

Keith and David have a game of racquetball (squash) together, after which Keith invites him to come along to his niece's birthday party. Parker tells Claire what happened to Andy – apparently he was smoking 'fry' (dope soaked in embalming fluid). Suddenly Claire realises that when Gabe was in the Fisher & Sons prep room, he stole some embalming fluid to concoct this potent yet extremely expensive drug. She's infuriated that he's let her down again.

Arriving at his niece Taylor's apartment, Keith is livid to discover that his sister Karla hasn't organised a birthday party for her daughter. Keith finds Karla passed out in her bedroom. Keith angrily accuses his sister of being back on drugs, but she strongly denies it, saying she's been clean for seven months now. Keith doesn't believe her, and they have a huge argument. He leaves, promising Taylor that he'll come back soon and take her to the movies.

Brenda's big dinner party starts off very well. Trevor and his wife Dawn are both gorgeous and great company, and their toddler son Will is cute but hyperactive. However, despite all trying to get along, it becomes clear that they will never have enough in common to become good friends again. As her guests leave, Brenda confesses to Nate that she loathed Trevor and baby Will, but quite liked Dawn. Nate suggests that perhaps they need to get to know more couples as friends. Brenda agrees, and contemplates taking up some kind of voluntary work to get things started. Brenda begins to worry that she may actually be a 'borderline' personality. 'I have no idea who I am,' she says.

The next day, Ruth demands to know from her sons where the $93,000 she lent them has gone. At that moment, the boys are shocked to discover that Appleby Caskets, who installed the new coffin wall, have been bought out by Kroehner and that Mitzi has given them the wall as 'a freebie'.

Rico is furious when he finds out that Vanessa has found the extra $11,000 for the deposit on the house by borrowing it from her sister Angelica. Vanessa accuses him of macho posturing and although he's still mad at her, he agrees not to pull out of the house purchase. At school, Claire finally catches up with Gabe and challenges him about the theft of the embalming fluid. Gabe confesses to stealing it and tells Claire about the videotape of the robbery, breaking down in tears. He goes down on his knees and begs Claire not to dump him, but she's finally had enough and walks away.

Nate starts to face his fear of death – literally – by looking straight at the ghost of Josh Langmead and deciding not to put his life in still more danger by going running again. He then finds David and sits down with him, telling his brother about his AVM. David holds Nate's hand as he sobs uncontrollably.

THE PRODIGAL SON

The death of Josh Langmead brings Nate's own mortality into sharp focus – Josh was a young, fit, healthy man who died because something went wrong in his brain. Throughout the episode Nate keeps ignoring 'Josh' – it's only when he literally faces him at the end that Nate gets the courage to deal with his AVM and tell David about the condition. The brothers' touching final scene is genuinely moving and proves once and for all that Nate really is different from the rest of the Fishers – David or Ruth would have taken *much* longer to break down and admit that they needed help.

ANAL CONTROL FREAK

David begins to work his way back into Keith's life in 'Out Out, Brief Candle' in a subtle way. Instead of making a direct play for Keith, he just ensures that he's around as a friend, playing racquetball and being willing to go along to Taylor's birthday party. Very sensible!

MOMMY, DEAREST

Ruth is still desperate to know about David's lifestyle, so becoming close friends with Robbie is probably almost as good in her eyes. She is totally amazed by her visit to Robbie's graduation ceremony, astonished at just how open people can be about their lives and their problems. All of these people seem to be moving forward with their lives, rebuilding them in a way that they want, so it's easy to see just how attractive this programme might appear to Ruth.

TEENAGE KICKS

After weeks of seeing the warning signs, Claire finally discovers just how messed up Gabe really is. Not only has he been making and selling the lucrative yet extremely dangerous 'fry' but he also stole embalming fluid from right under Claire's nose in order to complete the 'recipe'. Realising that his selfish behaviour indirectly caused Andy's spectacular breakdown, Claire finally decides that she's had enough and turns her back – literally – on Gabe.

DREAM ON, DREAMER

Nate's visions of Josh Langmead represent his own mind's struggle at coming to terms with his potentially fatal illness. Josh pops up at regular intervals, usually in tears, angry and scared at how unfair his early death was.

SOUNDTRACK

Ike and Tina Turner – 'You Shoulda Treated Me Right' (Mitzi arrives at work)

Mendelssohn – 'Opus 44, No.1- Andante'/Mendelssohn – 'Opus 12 – Canzonetta'/Mozart – 'Mento No. 2 In B Flat Major-Larghetto' (David and Nate consider buying the casket wall)

Mystic – 'Ghetto Birds' (Gabe and Claire talk in the high school parking lot)

Aim – 'Good Disease'/Goldfrapp – 'Pilots' (Brenda prepares Dinner)

SEX, DRUGS AND ROCK 'N' ROLL

We see the bizarre and scary side effects of smoking too many joints soaked in embalming fluid, and as a consequence it appears as though Andy will be in rehab for at least a week.

THE BRIGHT SIDE OF DEATH

Mitzi: Christmas came early. You're fired.
Gilardi: What?... Mitzi – just give me another chance!
Mitzi: You know, just cos I fucked you, that doesn't put us on a first-name basis...

Claire (to Andy): Woah! You're not on the list of people who get to touch my tits!

Mitzi (talking about her cup of coffee): You didn't put rat poison in here, did you?
Nate: Drink it and find out.

ISN'T THAT WHATSHISNAME?

Julie White (Mitzi Dalton Huntley) played Nadine Swoboda in the caustic comedy *Grace Under Fire*. **Alice Krige** (Alma) was the Borg Queen in the Star Trek movie *First Contact* and the TV series *Star Trek – Voyager*. **Nicki Micheaux** (Karla) appeared in the TV spin-off of the movie *Soul Food*, playing Lila. **Tuc Watkins** (Trevor) has worked on the soaps *Santa Barbara*, *One Life to Live* and *General Hospital* and played Mr Burns in the blockbuster movie *The Mummy* (Steven Sommers, 1999). **Judith Hoag** (Dawn) played news reporter April O'Neil in the first *Teenage Mutant Ninja Turtles* movie (Steve Barron, 1990). **Eddie Jemison** (Casket Salesman) can be seen in the 2001 remake of *Ocean's Eleven* (Steven Soderbergh). **Julianna McCarthy** (Beatrice) played Liz Foster in *The Young and the Restless* from 1973-1988, and also appeared in the revival of *Dark Shadows* as Mrs. Sarah Loomis Johnson and as an 'expert' in *Starship Troopers* (Paul Verhoeven, 1997).

UNANSWERED QUESTIONS

✟ Is Gabe totally out of Claire's life now?
✟ What will Mitzi's next plan of attack be?
✟ Is Karla really back on drugs again?
✟ Will Ruth decide to join The Plan?

EULOGY

In 'Out, Out, Brief Candle' we get to see just how ruthless Mitzi

Dalton Huntley can be. She makes Matt Gilardi look like a rank amateur and promptly fires him – and boy, is she an entertaining monster to watch! Top marks to Julie White for creating *Six Feet Under*'s version of the Wicked Witch of the (deep) South. We also see Brenda's next attempt to discover why she's unhappy. She invites her first true love Trevor over for dinner along with his beautiful and talented wife and their cute son. However, this ideal of happy family life is an anathema to Brenda too. She's still searching for happiness – or more accurately, for a solution to her unhappiness – but she just doesn't know where to look.

EPISODE 16
THE PLAN

Directed by: Rose Troche
Written by: Kate Robin

GUEST CAST
Richard Jenkins as Nathaniel
Eric Balfour as Gabe
Alice Krige as Alma
Grant Show as Scott Axelrod
Joel Brooks as Robbie
Beverly Todd as Mrs Charles
Graham Jarvis as Bobo
David Norona as Gary Deitman
Aysia Polk as Taylor
Uncredited as Detective Reece

Mare Winningham as Eileen Piper
Nan Martin as Rita Piper
David Andrews as Michael Piper
Kristopher Logan as Jack
Jerry Hauck as Stan
Romy Rosemont as Professor
Michael Bolshever as Minister
Luck Hari as Tahira
Raymond O'Connor as Man on Phone
Kyra Groves as Nurse

Amy Wheaton as Female Student
Ben Parrillo as Plan Man
Herschel Bleefeld as Male Student
Barbara Gruen as Plan Woman 1
Bree Michael Warner as Plan Woman 2
Greg Shamie as Guy in Car

WHO'S THE STIFF?

Michael John Piper, 1952-2001: After a feverish final few minutes of hallucination, Michael passes away in his hospital bed, after his wife promises him that it's only his body that's going to die.

PLOT SUMMARY

David downloads some information on AVM from the internet for Nate, who is not particularly grateful for the info. Eileen Piper checks through the casket wall, seemingly having a conversation with the spirit of her dead husband Michael. She explains to David and Nate that she's psychic, and tells Nate that he has a lot of pain 'in' his mind, before rapidly changing that to 'on' his mind, before telling him that everything will be OK. Eileen gives Nate one of her cards that reads 'Spiritual Consultation and Past Life Regression'. Nate and David then talk about what they think will happen after they die. David says he believes in heaven and hell, and Nate confesses that he thinks he's felt his father around.

Ruth goes to a meeting of The Plan where she sees the charismatic presenter Alma. Alma tells Ruth that she has to 'get out of bed' and see things the way they are so she can begin renovating her life.

Claire sees Gary Deitman and tells him that she hasn't seen Gabe in two weeks. She says it's so unfair that she's in love with someone so messed up. She thought that maybe she would be important to Gabe, but that's not the case any more.

Nate and David go to a meeting of the local independent funeral directors, including the spitting Bobo. They share horror stories of the way in which Kroehner has tried to put them all out of business. Nate's passionate belief in the small business rather than corporate values makes him a hero to the group. Claire is called back into Gary Deitman's office, where Detective Reece questions her about Gabe's disappearance and whether she has access to embalming fluid.

Brenda has decided to go back to school and is trying to choose which part-time class to take. Nate tries to initiate sex, but Brenda pushes him away. It's been nearly four weeks since they last made love, and Nate's getting concerned – they've only been together for seven months. Brenda insists that it's just a 'standard ebb' in their relationship.

Ruth gets home late from The Plan and talks with Claire about her experience. Although it was 'horrible', she says she's going to go back because she doesn't want to be rude. Even though she didn't enjoy the meeting, Ruth is already starting to use terminology and phrases from The Plan, which freak Claire out somewhat.

Nate asks Rico about his relationship with Vanessa and if they still have regular sex. He shocks Nate by saying that after Vanessa gave birth they went down to maybe 'three or four times a week'! David and Keith play another game of racquetball. Keith is worried that his sister may be using drugs again. He also mentions a few things that Eddie and he don't enjoy together – such as racquetball – which David is secretly delighted to hear.

Brenda goes to her first bio-genetics lecture. The professor is clearly threatened by Brenda's intelligence and is rude to her, resulting in Brenda walking out.

Eileen Piper speaks with Nate. He asks her if she has a sense of his father around, but she says no – but because of all the spirits in this room, she might have missed him. She does mention that there will be a child at Fisher & Sons very soon. At Michael Piper's service, Nathaniel tells Nate that he's been hanging around for so long just to get Nate 'prepared'. David then shocks Nate by telling him that rabidly anti-Kroehner Bobo has sold out to them.

Keith is shocked when he speaks to Taylor – she claims that Karla hasn't been home for three days. Keith's mom, who's looking after Taylor for a few days, tells Keith not to worry, everything's fine. Keith tells his mother that covering up for Karla isn't doing her any good.

Brenda, meanwhile, is having a drink in a bar on her own when a man tries to pick her up. She introduces herself as Candice. His name is Scott Axelrod. They flirt outrageously with each other and Scott gives her his card, hoping to take her out for dinner, just as Nate arrives. At The Plan, Ruth is having difficulty with the project, despite Robbie's encouragements. He tells Ruth to call Claire, to try and 'rebuild the foundations' of their relationship. She tells Claire that she wishes she could confide in her and that she loves her. As Robbie gets out of earshot, Ruth hangs up the call she made to the operator...

Meanwhile, Claire gets a call from Gabe, who asks her to come and get him. Brenda and Nate are having dinner, sharing their problems about the day – academia and psychics. Brenda tells Nate that she definitely doesn't believe in an afterlife – you can only live on through your relationships with others. It's an awkward conversation. She says she's prepared to die ever since she was six years old when she read a report on nuclear war. 'I wake up every day pretty surprised that everything's still here.' When Nate says he's surprised how she can live like that, Brenda tells him she assumed everyone thought like that.

At The Plan, Ruth is having great difficulty fitting in. She finally explodes at Alma, telling her and the rest of the attendees what a waste of time she thinks this is. They all burst into a round of applause – Ruth has finally reached the first step on her plan!

Claire picks up Gabe, who is angry, frustrated and full of self-pity. He's high, and wants Claire to drive him somewhere where he can chill out. She tells him to turn himself into the police. Just at that moment, a guy pulls up in the car next to them and starts coming on to Claire. Gabe pulls out a gun and shoots at him. Claire, hysterical, drives away, screaming at Gabe that she can't help him any more. She tries to go back to see if the other driver was hurt, grabs Gabe's gun and tells him to get out of the car. He takes her mobile phone and runs away into the night.

David and Nate are cleaning up the slumber room when Claire returns, crying. Ruth and Robbie share a post-Plan drink together. She thanks him for inviting her along to the meeting – he says not to bother thanking him, just to change. They laugh hysterically together. Keith has come to the house to talk to Claire. He takes Gabe's gun away. She gives Keith some information and they get ready to drive down to the station. She doesn't want to betray Gabe, but realises that something needs to be done before anyone else gets hurt.

THE PRODIGAL SON

Nate is still not very comfortable dealing with his illness – indeed, he even turns his nose up at the information that David downloads from the net for him. At the same time, Nate's having to deal with Brenda's odd behaviour. Their relationship has always involved a very healthy sex life (in fact, it began in a broom cupboard at the airport!), but now Brenda appears to be uninterested in sex it's beginning to unsettle Nate. Of course, Brenda is still trying to discover what's important in her life – but surely flirting and chatting up a complete stranger in a bar can't be healthy for her and Nate's relationship...

MOMMY, DEAREST

By deciding to join The Plan, Ruth makes a conscious decision to open up, to reveal her innermost feelings, and to be honest with people about how they make her feel. Of course, despite her best intentions it's not easy to rewrite a lifetime of repression in a few moments. Ruth so wants to be able to rebuild her life, but when the opportunity is presented to her, she continually chooses not to – for instance, pretending to telephone Claire. When Ruth finally blows her top at Alma and the rest of the members of The Plan, she thinks she's giving them a savaging, so it's quite a blow when she realises that losing her temper is actually the first step towards the rebuilding process. Poor Ruth!

TEENAGE KICKS

Claire's fears about Gabe come to a very unpleasant conclusion in 'The Plan'. Seeing her former boyfriend wired and out of control is bad enough, but when Gabe pulls out a gun and starts shooting at a nearby motorist, Claire realises that she has to put a stop to things. She confesses to Nate, David and Keith that she still loves Gabe very much – if she didn't love him, her actions would be so much less difficult. She finally agrees to go with Keith to the police station and make a statement to them about Gabe's actions, something she perhaps should have done some time before when she discovered his involvement in the robbery of the convenience store.

DREAM ON, DREAMER

Nate speaks to his father about where Michael Piper might be. He says that he has no answers – you'll never know until it happens to you. Nathaniel later asks David if he thinks he is in heaven or hell. Nathaniel reckons he's in hell – telling David that looking on the bright side, at least he'll have a familiar face waiting for him.

SOUNDTRACK

Schubert – 'Opus 29, No. 1, Andante' (Eileen Piper picks a coffin)
Roy Kohn – 'Young Girl' (Funeral directors' lunch)
Andy Caldwell – 'Invierno' (Brenda decides not to have sex with Nate)
Joel Evans – 'Somewhere In A Dream' (Brenda flirts at the bar)
Built to Spill – 'You Were Right' (Claire gets a call from a distraught Gabe)
Meeting Minds – 'Strong Nature' (Brenda and Nate together in the restaurant)
Custom – 'Hey Mister' (Claire picks up Gabe)
Wayne Hancock – 'Man Of The Road' (Ruth and Robbie at the bar)

THE BRIGHT SIDE OF DEATH

David: The thought of Mom getting self-actualised is kinda making me nauseous.

Nate: Are you sure it's not just the thought of Mom pissing into a jar?

Ruth: Fuck this. Fuck you. Fuck all of you, with your snivelling self-pity. And fuck *you*, Robbie, for dragging me to this terrible place and not letting me have a Snickers bar!

ISN'T THAT WHATSHISNAME?

Grant Show (Scott Axelrod) is another previous resident of *Melrose Place*. Fans of the TV show *Fame* might recognise **Graham Jarvis** (Bobo), who played Mr Dyrenforth in the last few seasons of the series. Actress, folk singer and former contestant on *The Gong Show* **Mare Winningham** (Eileen Piper) played Dr Amanda Lee in the fifth series of *ER* and had a small role in the mini-series *The Thorn Birds*, though it's probably for her part in brat-pack classic *St Elmo's Fire* (Joel Schumacher, 1985) that she's best remembered. **Nan Martin** (Rita Piper) has the rare honour of having played the mother of serial killer Freddie Kruger, as revealed in *A Nightmare On Elm Street 3: Dream Warriors* (Chuck Russell, 1987). She was also a regular on *The Drew Carey Show* and can be seen in the films *Cast Away* (Robert Zemeckis, 2000) and *Shallow Hal* (the Farrelly brothers, 2001). **David Andrews** (Michael Piper) appeared in *Apollo 13* (Ron Howard, 1995), *Fight Club* (David Fincher, 1999) and *Hannibal* (Ridley Scott, 2001) as well as the TV shows *Murder One* and *From the Earth to the Moon*. **Luck Hari** (Tahira) popped up as the cafe waitress in the first four years of *Frasier*. **Raymond O'Connor** (Man on Phone) will not be recognisable to fans of *Buffy*, though they might recall he played a loan shark in the episode 'Tabula Rasa' – and by 'shark', I mean finned, toothy and smelling of fish! **Amy Wheaton** (Female Student) is the younger sister of *Star Trek – The Next Generation* actor Wil Wheaton.

UNANSWERED QUESTIONS

✞ Where has Karla gone?

✝ Is Gabe gone for good?

✝ Will Brenda cheat on Nate with Scott Axelrod? Why has she gone off sex? Is it just sex with Nate that she's bored with?

EULOGY

Along with Billy's attack on Brenda in 'A Private Life', the sequence where Gabe holds Claire at gunpoint is one of the scariest moments in *Six Feet Under*. The often overlooked Eric Balfour puts in a fantastic performance as Gabe's life crumbles around him, but Lauren Ambrose really steals the acting honours as Claire tries to balance the love she has for Gabe with the knowledge that she *has* to turn him in. Meanwhile we are treated to quite simply the funniest moment in the entire series so far, as Ruth's precious veneer of respectability is shattered. Remember how she often reprimands her family for their bad language? Well, when she unleashes a torrent of foul four-letter words on the pompous members of The Plan, it's a moment that neither she nor viewers will ever forget!

EPISODE 17
DRIVING MR MOSSBANK

Directed by: Michael Cuesta
Written by: Rick Cleveland

GUEST CAST
Lili Taylor as Lisa
Joanna Cassidy as Margaret
Grant Show as Scott Axelrod
David Norona as Gary Deitman
Aysia Park as Taylor
Beverly Todd as Mrs Charles
Kellie Waymire as Melissa
Eric Bruskotter as Keith's Partner

Mike McCafferty as Adam Mossbank
Judy Prescott as Kimberley Mossbank
Hansford Rowe as Harold Mossbank
Deborah Theaker as Tour Guide

WHO'S THE STIFF?

Harold Mossbank, 1932-2001: Fades away whilst enjoying a coach tour of Seattle.

PLOT SUMMARY

Claire chats with Gary Deitman – she's furious at him for allowing the police to crash their last session. She hasn't heard from Gabe since the night of the gun incident. David has an induction meeting with Harold Mossbank's children Adam and Kimberley. They tell him that they want their father's body driven back down from Seattle to Los Angeles – he never flew anywhere. Nate agrees to fly up to Seattle, hire a van, and then drive the already embalmed Mr Mossbank back to LA. He also offers to pay for Claire to travel with him, as he really needs the company.

Keith's mom is going home for a few days to be with her husband whilst he has a hernia operation. Karla is nowhere to be found, so Keith agrees to look after Taylor. During a family meal, Ruth enquires about David's love life, and then wonders why she hasn't seen Gabe around for a while. Claire tells Ruth that he joined the Hare Krishnas!

Nate tells Brenda that he's going up to Seattle, but questions why he never asked Brenda to go with him first. She tells Nate that it's not weird at all, but still rejects his overtures towards making love.

On the plane to Seattle, Claire asks Nate if he asked her along to distract her from worrying about Gabe. He says no – he just thought it would be fun. Their plan is to stay with one of Nate's old Seattle friends, Lisa. He protests that they were never an item, but clams up when Claire asks Nate if he and Lisa ever 'did it'. Arriving at Lisa's house, Claire is immediately taken by how outgoing and effusive Lisa is – she's a real Seattle hippy chick.

Ruth phones Hiram to let him know about her new 'Life Blueprint' (courtesy of The Plan). She tells him that she harbours no hard feelings towards him, but when he asks if she wants to get back with him, she says, 'You know something Hiram? Fuck off!' She then phones her old 'friend' Amelia (who she lost all the money at the races with) and tells her she is happy to renew their friendship if she wants. Next on her list is her sister Sarah: she leaves an answerphone message asking her to get back in touch because there are things she still needs to sort out.

Keith phones David and asks him to pick up Taylor from school at 3pm. David jumps at the chance to help Keith out.

Lisa updates Nate on how the Co-op is functioning without him. It seems to be going very well indeed, and Lisa says that everyone misses him. Lisa is surprised that Nate is still with Brenda – eight months is a record for him! Because he is in an awkward place with Brenda right now, he doesn't feel able to open up. Lisa tells Nate that she's been offered a job in LA, working as a vegan chef for a film company. She doesn't know if she'll take the job, as LA is such a 'godless place' and because they use animal products in the film. Claire uses a trip to the bathroom as an opportunity to flush away the tofu meatloaf she tried to eat. Later, Nate admits to Claire that he and Lisa were indeed 'fuck-buddies' – they were just friends who occasionally slept together, and Lisa was always aware of the boundaries.

Brenda is working on a new client – Melissa, who confesses that her job is as a prostitute. Brenda is quietly impressed! As Melissa leaves, Brenda gets a call from her mother Margaret, who is in a hysterical state. She meets her mother outside the Tranquillity Spa – Margaret is convinced that Bernard is inside the spa with another woman, but Brenda tells her not to get so worked up. So what if her father is having an affair?

Whilst Nate is trying to order some burgers from a drive-thru, he suddenly loses control of what he's saying, then has to get out of the rented van to vomit. He's deeply worried by what's happening. He lets Claire drive whilst he gets some fresh air and makes a phone call to his doctor in Los Angeles. Meanwhile, Margaret and Brenda are sitting waiting outside the Tranquillity Spa to see if Bernard will come out with a young woman. Margaret tells Brenda that she's not angry he's sleeping with another woman, she's angry that he didn't tell her first. Brenda is amazed when Margaret lists a whole series of rules that she and Bernard have for playing away from home.

David is having trouble with the surprisingly potty-mouthed Taylor. She keeps misbehaving until she wanders down into the preparation room and sees Rico and David working on a corpse. She is fascinated, and David finds a way to bond with her. In Seattle, Nate tells Claire about his AVM. What he's just experienced is a mild seizure – he tells her it's no big deal and he doesn't want Ruth to know because she'd 'spaz out'. Claire doesn't believe Nate's story that it's nothing to worry about, and Nate tells her not to tell David what happened.

Margaret sees a woman coming out of the spa and getting into Bernard's car. She goes to speak to the woman, but very soon starts pulling her hair and trying to drag her out of the car window. 'Hope you like herpes!' she shouts as the woman drives off. A stunned Brenda asks why she needed to be here to witness that little outburst. They have a huge argument. 'You've spent 32 years being your little brother's nursemaid to avoid having any emotional life of your own.' Their argument spirals further and further out of control until Brenda viciously slaps Margaret across the face and Margaret throws her out of her car in tears.

At the dinner table, Taylor confides in Ruth and David that she doesn't really like Eddie much. When Keith finally arrives to collect Taylor, David tells Keith that it was no trouble looking after her.

Claire finds Lisa on her hands and knees in her kitchen, trying to reason with some ants that they should leave her house. Lisa admits to Claire that she used to be in love with Nate, but she isn't any more. They have a heart-to-heart about how much better off they are without men. Nate is outside Lisa's house on the phone to Brenda. Their conversation is stilted, but they both are able to say that they miss each other. As she hangs up, Brenda starts to cry. She then gets into her bath and fantasises about Scott Axelrod making love to her. Lisa brings Nate an extra blanket to keep him warm. He breaks down, sobbing hysterically. Lisa comforts him. The next morning as Nate and Claire are leaving, Nate leaves one of his shirts for her to remember him by.

Ruth finally gets round to voicing her fears to David. She tells him that Taylor is young and impressionable, and that he should avoid confusing the young girl by being blatant about his and Keith's former relationship in front of her. David says he's happy that The Plan is helping Ruth to rebuild her life, but tells her to keep that 'fucking shit' to herself in future as she's beginning to sound like a crazy person.

THE PRODIGAL SON

A lovely trip back to his old stomping ground of Seattle turns nasty for Nate as he suffers his first major AVM seizure. To say that he is freaked out by the attack is an understatement – he's terrified. Nate really wishes that he could be at home with Brenda, but as their relationship is in such an awkward place, it's Lisa that he ends up turning to for comfort.

ANAL CONTROL FREAK

David seizes his chance to get closer to Keith by agreeing to spend time with Taylor. However, David is surprised by how much he enjoys having her around – despite her bad language and forthright nature. It's still a little worrying to see how determined David is to get back with Keith – after all, Keith is in a relationship with someone else. Furthermore, if there's one lesson we've already learned from *Six Feet Under*, it's that relationships can only ever work if both parties are already happy and content with their own lives. At this stage it appears that David believes he can only ever be happy if he's reunited with his ex-boyfriend.

MOMMY, DEAREST

Ruth's attempts to get her life under control meet with varied success in this episode. She makes a final break from Hiram, and she attempts to rebuild her relationship with her hippy sister Sarah, someone she has been out of contact with for many years. However, despite her attempts to be seen as understanding and tolerant towards David's sexuality, she makes a huge mistake. When Ruth voices her concern that young Taylor should not be raised by gay men because of the 'confusion' it may cause her, David snaps. The Plan may have encouraged Ruth to speak exactly what's on her mind, but going from one extreme (total repression) to another (total openness) carries its own risks too.

DREAM ON, DREAMER

Brenda has a highly erotic dream about Scott Axelrod, the man she met in the bar in 'The Plan'. She imagines him turning up at her house and giving her oral sex. It's clear that Brenda isn't satisfied with her relationship with Nate...

SOUNDTRACK

Vienna – 'Where I Wanna Be' (Keith talks to his mother)
Yo La Tengo – 'Our Way To Fall' (Nate and Claire arrive at Lisa's)
Sarah Harmer – 'Basement Apt' (Eating vegan meatloaf)
Neotropic – 'Neotropic' (Nate calls his doctor)
Joe 90 – 'Drive' (Nate and Claire drive away)

SEX, DRUGS AND ROCK 'N' ROLL

Brenda's dream about Scott Axelrod is enough to make even the most open-minded blush. For heaven's sake, woman – you're meant to be in a relationship!

THE BRIGHT SIDE OF DEATH

Margaret: Brenda, just because your parents are shrinks doesn't mean you know anything about psychology.
Brenda: Yeah, and just because you're a shrink doesn't mean you're not out of your fucking mind.

Taylor to David: 'I guess that makes you a punk-ass fudge-packer too?'

ISN'T THAT WHATSHISNAME?

The sublime **Lili Taylor** (Lisa) has often been linked to that 80s Brat-pack that saw the rise of John Cusack and Molly Ringwald. She appeared alongside Cusack in *Say Anything* (Cameron Crowe, 1989) and *High Fidelity* (2000) and her other films include *Ransom* (Ron Howard, 1996), *The Haunting* (Jan de Bont, 1998) and *Pecker* (John Waters, 1998). **Kellie Waymire** (Melissa) has recently 'boldly gone' with the crew of *Enterprise*, playing Crewman Elizabeth Cutler. **Eric Bruskotter** (Keith's Partner) was also a regular in the TV dramas *Providence* and *Tour of Duty*, while his movie work includes *Starship Troopers* (Paul Verhoeven, 1997) and two of the *Major League* sequels.

UNANSWERED QUESTIONS

✟ Is The Plan really the best way for Ruth to rebuild her life, or will it result in her losing more than she gains?
✟ Is this the end of Bernard and Margaret Chenowith's marriage – and if so, will anybody care?
✟ Now that Nate has had a major seizure, will he go through with one of the different surgical options open to him?
✟ Will Keith be able to handle Taylor?

EULOGY

'Driving Mr Mossbank' is a very different type of episode than we've been used to. Relocating a lot of the action from Los Angeles to Seattle really does change the pace of the programme and it's a refreshing shift in focus. Lili Taylor makes a memorable guest appearance as one of Nate's old flames, and it's fun to speculate what Nate's life might have been like if he'd returned to Seattle after Nathaniel's funeral. It's also fantastic to see more of Joanna Cassidy as Margaret Chenowith, a woman who brings entirely new meaning to the term 'oddball'.

EPISODE 18
THE INVISIBLE WOMAN

Directed by: Jeremy Podeswa
Written by: Bruce Eric Kaplan

GUEST CAST
Kelly Waymire as Melissa
Marina Black as Parker McKenna
Aysia Polk as Taylor
David Norona as Gary Deitman
Adam Scott as Ben Cooper
Tim Maculan as Father Jack
Terrell Clayton as Eddie
Eric Bruskotter as Keith's Partner

Christine Estabrook as Emily Previn
Brad Greenquist as Building Manager
David Raibon as Junkie Man
Jamie Brown as Junkie Woman
Heather McPhaul as Proctor 1
Bob Rumnock as Proctor 2
Bhavana Kundanmal as Parker Imposter
Bill Kalmenson as Businessman
Aysia Lee as Needs a Pencil

WHO'S THE STIFF?

Emily Previn, 1954-2001: Chokes to death whilst eating a healthy and nutritious meal. As Emily lived alone, it is a week before her body is discovered, smelling rotten and covered in ants.

PLOT SUMMARY

Brenda has decided to write a book, much to Nate's bemusement. 'Charlotte finally speaks – the story of your fucked-up childhood, but from your point of view'. Instead, Brenda says that it's going to be fiction. She jokes that Nate might be in the book 'if you ever do anything interesting'.

At school, Claire is chatting with her friend Parker McKenna. She's written a list of the most attractive male members of staff. Parker instantly puts Claire's counsellor Gary on her list, saying that she could easily fuck him. That afternoon, Claire tells Gary that she's going to sit her SATs that weekend. Gary is delighted that she's deciding to knuckle down. He says he's aware that she's scared of people being able to see the real her.

Nate and David are going through Emily Previn's details. She had prearranged all of her details a few years before, detailing the precise arrangements for her own funeral. David tells Nate that he had fun doing his own! They discover that Emily didn't have anyone that she really cared about – no relatives, no friends, no work colleagues who cared enough about her to come to the funeral.

Brenda is sitting at her laptop, trying to write, when words of derision and demotivation appear on the screen. David has a date with lawyer Ben Cooper – he's a bit nervous and tries to end the date early, but the guy is actually really interested in him.

Keith is still having problems with Taylor. He suggests that they both ease up on each other. Eddie is very understanding, but Keith is worried that he's behaving like his father. When Eddie tries to get intimate with Keith, he pushes him away.

Ruth dreams that her house is completely empty. She walks through the house until she sees herself asleep, then shouts at herself to get up, which is exactly the point when she does wake up, surrounded by all of her normal furniture. Brenda is still not having much luck with her writing, so she phones up Melissa, her massage client, and arranges to meet for lunch.

Rico is deeply nauseated by the week-old corpse of Emily Previn. It's going to take a lot of work to get her ready for a viewing. Nate wonders if Emily was a twisted, evil woman – maybe that's why she had no friends. But Rico says she was OK – even in death, you can tell what a person was like.

It's time for the SATs, and Claire is horrified when another girl arrives and signs in for the exam as 'Parker McKenna' – it's clear that this is why Parker wasn't stressing out over taking the test. When Claire finally meets her real friend again, she tells Parker that she's disgusted by her cheating and informs her that she doesn't want to speak to her again.

Brenda's lunch with Melissa reveals a lot about how she's feeling about Nate. She tells Melissa that 'it's really sad that you can love somebody so much and still have no idea what's really going on in their head'. She adds that if she really did know, then there's the likelihood that she would dump Nate. Melissa and Brenda's lunch actually goes really well – they are both grateful that the other doesn't treat them like a freak. Brenda is really impressed that there isn't a touch of victim about Melissa – it's almost as though being a prostitute has empowered her.

Nate and Ruth decide to go to Emily's house to collect an outfit for her to be buried in, as the clothes she arrived in had rotted. Ruth really wants to pick out a nice outfit for Emily – it's the least she can do. Looking round Emily's apartment, Ruth feels really sorry for this lonely woman.

Keith moans to his partner about the way in which Eddie doesn't understand that now he's looking after Taylor he has other responsibilities. As his partner is offering some sound advice, they hear the sounds of a heated domestic argument. The woman is screaming and crying for the man (presumably her boyfriend or husband) to leave her alone. The man pulls a gun on her and demands that he listen to her. Keith and his partner rush over to help the woman. Keith tells the man to put his gun down, but instead the man swings round towards Keith, gun outstretched. Keith shoots the man, who goes down instantly. The woman is horrified, shouting at Keith,

'What's wrong with you? What did you do that for?' Keith's partner reassures him that he did the right thing.

On his second date with Ben, David confesses that he is a funeral director. He admits that he lied about his job because he didn't want to scare Ben off. He realises that now he really likes Ben, he has to tell the truth. Ben thinks it's really cute, and they kiss. Back at home, David is feeling really happy over his new relationship when Keith knocks at the door – he's come over because he's shattered over having killed somebody. They kiss passionately.

Next morning, Rico is angry. He worked late on Emily Previn but despite all of his efforts he wasn't able to do an effective reconstruction. He feels guilty about letting her down. David is woken up by a call from Keith – which shocks him because he thought Keith was still in bed with him. Keith is very dismissive. He's in a relationship, and he thinks that their night of passion was a mistake. He tells David that they shouldn't see each other any more.

Melissa gets a phone call from one of her colleagues, who says she can't work with Melissa as a 'watcher' that afternoon (that is sitting in the room watching Melissa and her client having sex). Brenda, intrigued by the concept, agrees to stand in on this occasion. Going through with it, Brenda is strangely liberated and excited by the danger and seediness of the experience. Claire, still furious, is in Gary's office. She is mad that after all the effort she put in, someone else has cheated and managed to achieve a positive result. Gary is concerned that she is using someone else's issues to transfer her own concerns. Claire is then even more shocked when Gary says that he is aware of the 'sexual tension' between Claire and himself, but it would be unprofessional and inappropriate for anything to be acted upon.

Emily Previn's viewing is as empty as predicted. Ruth turns up for the service, and ensures that there's a decent turnout by grabbing David, Rico and Claire to take part. She even invites Father Jack to conduct the service. Father Jack's eulogy is quite inspiring. He says that everyone who comes into your life affects it in some way – it's your job to interpret how it affects it. After the service, Father Jack catches up with David – he's delighted to see him, and tells David that he really affected his life. When David asks how, he says he'll tell him another time.

Ruth tells her children that the reason she's upset about Emily Previn is that she doesn't want to be strangers with her family. She tries to force them to be 'intimate' with her but Nate protests that it should really happen organically. Ruth turns and leaves, saying that she hopes it happens before she goes the way of Emily. The next morning, Ruth makes herself a cup of tea and looks at all the photos of her children on the mantelpiece. She breaks down and cries.

Brenda tells Nate that something has been on her mind. She presents Nate with an engagement ring and asks him to marry her. It's a rather ugly ring – it was her grandfather's fraternity ring. She tells Nate that she wouldn't know what to do if he left her. Nate replies by saying he's not going anywhere, that he loves her, and that yes, they will get married!

ANAL CONTROL FREAK

After a long dry period, David ends up getting attention from two people at once – new potential boyfriend Ben and his old flame Keith. Ben seems to be absolutely perfect for David – intelligent, funny and completely smitten. He even forgives David for the little white lie he told about his job, thinking that it's quite cute. Everything seems to be going really well until the shocked and upset Keith suddenly shows up at David's and they have a night of passion. It's understandable behaviour from Keith, considering the trauma he's gone through at work and the lack of support he's getting from his boyfriend Eddie, but the impact that this night of passion has on David is immense. When Keith tells him the next day that it was a big mistake to get back together, poor David is left reeling from a massive collision of mixed feelings.

MOMMY, DEAREST

Ruth is still trying to rebuild her life through The Plan, but when she leans about the tragic demise of lonely Emily Previn, it really hits her hard. Ruth sees herself in Emily – a woman abandoned by people and left to deal with life alone. It's a very scary prospect and one that Ruth will stop at nothing to try to avoid.

TEENAGE KICKS

We see yet another aspect to Claire in 'The Invisible Woman' – a hatred of injustice and unfair behaviour. Claire has really worked hard to motivate herself into working for her SAT exams, but to discover Parker cheating really hits her hard. It's a betrayal of everything that she's trying to do to improve her life, and to have that betrayal come from her friend is an extra slap in the face.

DREAM ON, DREAMER

Ruth imagines herself walking around her house – not only is it empty of her family, it's also been completely stripped of all the furniture, nick-nacks and possessions. It's a frightening insight into how Ruth has been affected by the death of Emily Previn. She desperately doesn't want to be left alone, but is scared that the more she forces her children to be 'intimate' with her, the more she will push them away.

SOUNDTRACK

Banx De France – 'Sex In The Machine' (David's first date with Ben)
Llorca featuring Lady Bird – 'My Precious Thing' (David and Ben have their first kiss)
Alexkid – 'I Think (Dorfmeister & Alexkid Dub)' (Brenda 'watches' Melissa with a client)
Peter Krause – 'And I'm Telling You I'm Not Going' (from the musical Dreamgirls) (Nate's rock fantasy)

SEX, DRUGS AND ROCK 'N' ROLL

David gets a surprising reunion with Keith, despite having only just started seeing Ben! Brenda also gets a surprise when she volunteers to sit in on one of Melissa's 'tricks' and watch them having sex. Although she doesn't take part in a physical sense, Brenda is still there – invisible, you might say.

THE BRIGHT SIDE OF DEATH

Ruth: Won't *any* of you have intimacy with me?

Brenda: Nate Fisher – would you be my wife?

ISN'T THAT WHATSHISNAME?

Christine Estabrook (Emily Previn) had a small role in *The Usual Suspects* (Bryan Singer, 1995). **Brad Greenquist** (Building Manager) played Victor Pascow, a student who meets an unfortunate end but refuses to die in Stephen King's *Pet Sematary* (Mary Lambert, 1989).

UNANSWERED QUESTIONS

✝ How exactly did David inspire Father Jack? Has the priest actually come out?
✝ Will getting engaged put a stop to Brenda's increasingly erratic behaviour?

EULOGY

The 'Invisible Woman' of the title is of course not just Emily Previn – it could equally apply to both Ruth and Brenda. Ruth is doing her best to keep her family together, but the terrifying prospect of dying alone with nobody to mourn her passing shakes her to her very core. She knows that she's running the risk of pushing the people she loves still further away, but she just can't help herself.

Another person running the risk of loneliness is Brenda. She seems almost determined to go down a road of sexual adventure and experimentation – something that you would not expect a woman in such a strong relationship to need to do. Any predictable person might have asked their partner for a bit more freedom or some time out if they felt constricted or constrained. Not Brenda. Instead she takes what appears to be a rather impulsive action and asks Nate to marry her. If she's concerned about her own happiness (which the evidence of the past few episodes would seem to suggest), then surely making a lifetime commitment to someone is the worst thing you could possibly do?

Despite these worries on Brenda's part, we as viewers find it difficult to be anything but overjoyed for *Six Feet Under*'s 'Odd Couple'. It's obvious just how well suited they are, but they are going to have to be a lot more honest with each other – and themselves – if their relationship is going to have any chance of surviving.

EPISODE 19
IN PLACE OF ANGER

Directed by: Michael Engler
Written by: Christian Taylor

GUEST CAST
Ed O'Ross as Nikolai
Julie White as Mitzi Dalton Huntley
Justina Machado as Vanessa
Adam Scott as Ben Cooper
Graham Jarvis as Bobo
Aysia Polk as Taylor
Terrell Clayton as Eddie
Ricardo Antonio Chavira as Ramon
Harriet Sansom Harris as Catherine Collins

Patricia Clarkson as Aunt Sarah
Steve Ryan as Matthew Collins
Gwendolyn Whiteside as Woman on Boat
Erik Stolhanske as Man on Boat
Leonard Kelly-Young as Inspector
Joshua Previn as Massage Client

WHO'S THE STIFF?

Matthew Heath Collins, 1959-2001: Fell overboard from his company's expensive party yacht the worse for wear from alcohol.

PLOT SUMMARY

Nate and Brenda spend a very happy morning following their first night of passion in weeks. Nate follows up Brenda's proposal by asking her to marry him, and he tells her that he loves her. She replies, 'Good.' Nate suggests that Brenda comes round to the Fishers' for a meal to tell them the good news. Ben has stayed over at David's again – they've been going out for three weeks now and things seem to be going well. Claire is surprised when she comes down for breakfast and sees Nikolai there too. Ruth mentions that Nate has asked everyone to be around for a big family dinner, as he has something important to tell everyone.

Nate and David hold Matthew Collins' intake meeting. His widow Catherine is very upset, feeling closer to her own mortality. She seems reluctant to commit to any kind of formal arrangement; David suggests she's shopping around for the best deal. David later finds out that Catherine has chosen to place the funeral with a Kroehner affiliate company, and he jumps to the conclusion that Mitzi Huntley is gunning for them again, which agitates him a great deal. Ruth is shocked when her sister Sarah turns up. Sarah is delighted to discover that Ruth did The Plan, and is taken by the artwork hanging in Claire's room. She tells Claire that she's an artist: 'You've got an eye – you see through the veil. It's a blessing and a curse.' Claire is quite enthralled by her.

Rico's new house is proving to be a money pit – water has seeped in and is causing structural problems. Vanessa and Rico argue about whose fault it was for buying the house. Mitzi gets a call telling her that Catherine Collins has switched her husband's funeral back to Fisher & Sons. She's intrigued, and decides to spend some more time with the 'fabulous Fisher boys'.

As Ruth and Claire prepare dinner, Nikolai and Sarah enjoy a Russian singalong. Sarah is entranced and whispers to Ruth how impressed she is with Nikolai: 'The sex must be amazing!' The family meal is highly entertaining, with people finding out lots about each other. Nate then announces that Brenda and he have gotten engaged. Everyone is delighted, except perhaps Ruth, who just seems shell-shocked. A drunken David gets back to his room just as Ben is calling. Ben is very supportive, but is curious as to why he didn't get invited to the big family meal if everyone else's partner is there. David just tells him that he was helping him avoid a horrible night. The following morning, Nate asks Ruth to support his decision to marry Brenda – she's the woman he loves, even if Ruth doesn't approve of her.

Mitzi calls on Fisher & Sons. She blackmails Nate and David to coming on a trip with her, which turns out to be on board a private jet along with their old 'anti-Kroehner' funeral director friend Bobo. They arrive at a palatial mansion in Palm Springs, formerly owned by Frank Sinatra, where Mitzi insists that they relax and have a good time. Mitzi significantly ups her offer to buy out Fisher & Sons, but Nate tears it up. On the plane on the way back to Los Angeles, David wonders whether they should have taken her up on her offer, but Nate strongly argues that they have to keep the business alive. Nate also lies to David, telling him that he confided in Brenda about his AVM about a week ago.

Brenda wakes up from a nightmare of Nate suffocating her with a pillow whilst simultaneously telling her 'I love you'. Brenda's client is a handsome man. Whilst massaging him, he gets an erection. Instead of ignoring it as she should, Brenda masturbates him to climax. Afterwards, she tells the client that he can't book any further appointments with her.

Catherine Collins, despite Nate's strong advice, demands to see her husband's body, which had been carved up by a motorboat's propellers. Her reaction is not what Nate expected. Catherine laughs hysterically at the corpse, saying how glad she is that her husband is dead because now he can't hit her any more. In David's room, he and Ben are kissing when Ben tells him, 'I could really love you, David Fisher!' David pulls away and confesses that he's still in love with someone else. Ben is angry that David never told him this, and walks out of his life.

Sarah and Ruth have an argument just as Sarah leaves. Sarah

accuses Ruth of martyrdom and Ruth accuses Sarah of never taking any responsibility and 'having more fun than I did!' Sarah confesses that she yearns for a baby she was unable to conceive, and surrounds herself with art and artists because she has no talent of her own. Acknowledging their differences, the two form an uneasy but slightly warmer friendship.

Following his encounter with Catherine, Nate asks Brenda to make sure she never stays with him if she's unhappy. She promises to leave him if she ever stops loving him. Ruth brings Claire a boxful of childhood paintings, models and toys that she made – it's a lovely moment of bonding between the two of them.

THE PRODIGAL SON

After weeks of worrying about his relationship with Brenda, we finally get to see a happy and upbeat Nate Fisher again. He's so proud when he announces the news to his family and refuses to let Ruth's surly behaviour put a dampener on proceedings. Nate continues to behave in a bullish fashion when dealing with Mitzi's latest attempt to buy the business. In fact, it's only when Nate deals with the near-hysterical Catherine Collins that he comes down from cloud nine for a while. Despite their outward appearances, the Collinses had a loveless marriage, one that failed to live up to its initial promise. So Nate speaks to Brenda and makes her promise that she will end the relationship if the love ever dies between them. Talk about tempting fate…

ANAL CONTROL FREAK

David comes to a realisation about his own life in this episode too. Despite having spent three weeks building a relationship with somebody who appears to be his perfect match, David decides to throw it all away. Either he's unable to move on from his past with Keith, or he genuinely thinks that he can exploit the difficulties in Eddie and Keith's relationship to muscle in himself. Whatever way, it seems a terrible shame that David has had to hurt Ben in the process of discovering what it is he really wants in life.

MOMMY, DEAREST

Although it's something that she was encouraged to do as part of The Plan, having a reunion with her sister Sarah is a big hurdle to overcome for Ruth. Ruth harbours lots of feelings of resentment and jealousy towards Sarah – she's always been the one who had fun, who lived her life, who experimented and tried new things. Ruth was the one who did her duty – got married, raised a family, supported the business. It comes as a big surprise to Ruth to discover that Sarah longed for many of the things that Ruth took for granted... a long-term relationship and children in particular. The parallels between Ruth/Sarah and David/Nate are poignantly clear to see. The grass is always greener on the other side of the fence, it seems.

DREAM ON, DREAMER

Brenda's disturbing dream of Nate strangling her whilst simultaneously saying 'I love you' is a clear indicator of how she views the idea of committing to one person.

SOUNDTRACK

Iffy – 'Super Bad Girl (Mint Royale Remix)' (The office boat party)
Patricia Clarkson & Ed O'Ross – 'Bublicki' (Nikolai and Sarah get drunk on vodka)
Mozart – 'Milan String Quartet #1 In A Major, Allegro' (Fisher family dinner)
Frank DeWolfe – 'Like A Friend' (In the plane on the way to Palm Springs)
Wanda De Sah – 'So Danco Samba (Jazz n' Samba)' (Mitzi shows off Kroehner's swanky house)

George Shearing – 'If I Should Lose You' (Mitzi propositions David and Nate in the hot tub)
John Beltran – 'Collage Of Dreams' (Brenda gives a client some extra 'service')
Royksopp – 'Sparks' (Nate and Brenda talk)

SEX, DRUGS AND ROCK 'N' ROLL

What on earth does Brenda think she's doing? She's only just asked Nate to marry her, and now she's introducing one of her clients to the pleasures of the palm...

THE BRIGHT SIDE OF DEATH

Sarah: I had a lover who was Russian. He once told me that vodka is to Russians as therapy is to Americans.
Brenda: Yeah, something habit forming and expensive that totally destroys your ability to lead an authentic life.

ISN'T THAT WHATSHISNAME?

Patricia Clarkson (Aunt Sarah) appeared in a run of episodes of *Frasier* in 2002 as Claire French and played Annie Hoffman in *Murder One*. She also played the governor's dying wife in the film adaptation of Stephen King's *The Green Mile* (Frank Darabond, 1999) and took the Piper Laurie role of the authoritarian mother in the 2002 TV remake of *Carrie*. **Steve Ryan** (Matthew Collins) played Officer Healy in the first few episodes of the first series of HBO's prison drama *Oz*.

UNANSWERED QUESTIONS

✠ Is this the start of a slippery slope for Brenda?
✠ Have Rico and Vanessa really bought a lemon of a house?

✝ Has David done a silly thing by breaking up with Ben?

EULOGY

We always suspected that there had to be a reason for Ruth's martyr syndrome and in 'In Place of Anger' we discover exactly what – or more accurately, who – that reason is. Sarah is the polar opposite of her sister, but despite what Ruth would have her family believe, she's no irresponsible monster. Sarah has a great deal of love and compassion within her, and has a burning need to be loved – just as much as Ruth does. Ruth's determination to protect her children from Sarah's 'corrupting' influence is so cleverly written that I'm sure many families will recognise a similar kind of scenario in their own brood!

Patricia Clarkson puts in a fantastic guest performance as Sarah, making her funny, vulnerable yet wise and warm at the same time – exactly the kind of person you'd love to have as a weird, disreputable auntie.

EPISODE 20
BACK TO THE GARDEN

Directed by: Daniel Attias
Written by: Jill Soloway

GUEST CAST
Patricia Clarkson as Aunt Sarah
Joanna Cassidy as Margaret
Molly Parker as Rabbi Ari
Ed O' Ross as Nikolai
Joel Brooks as Robbie
Justina Machado as Vanessa
Kellie Waymire as Melissa
Terrell Clayton as Eddie
Stark Sands as Toby
Ricardo Antonio Chavira as Ramon
Eric Bruskotter as Keith's Partner
Maria Carmen as Graciela

Sara Mornell as Jessica Shapiro
Lee Garlington as Fiona
Chris Ufland as Jeffrey Shapiro
Robert Pine as Basil
Brett Paesel as Gourd Woman
Tannoz Bahremand as Cantor
Ben Davis as Doctor
David Ackert as Truck Driver

Moira Price as Toby's Mom
Francisco Javier as Ramon's Buddy
Jeffrey Ross as Shiva Comic
Christi Lake as Porno Girl
Benjamin Banks as Porno Guy 1
Jason Dougherty as Porno Guy 2

WHO'S THE STIFF?

Jeffrey Marc Shapiro, 1963-2001: His masturbatory game-playing whilst watching a porn movie resulted in him dying from accidental auto-erotic asphyxia.

PLOT SUMMARY

Keith has begun dreaming of a reunion between himself and David –quite a shock for him as he is still with Eddie. Keith and Eddie have a big argument, which results in them breaking up and Eddie storming out. Despite Ruth's protestations, Claire decides to go ahead and visit her Aunt Sarah for the weekend.

It's the induction meeting for Jeff Shapiro. His wife is deeply upset by her husband's accidental suicide, and is keen to ensure that proper Jewish tradition is upheld and he is buried the next day. Margaret and Brenda meet up for a sushi lunch to toast Margaret and Bernard's marriage break-up. The woman Margaret attacked outside the spa has now moved in with Bernard. Brenda casually mentions that she's getting married to Nate, and Margaret is dismissive, thinking that Nate doesn't have enough brain power to keep her daughter happy. They share a few happy moments laughing and bitching at each other.

David is surprised when Keith phones to tell him that he's split up with Eddie. Not knowing what to say, David hangs up. Confused, he later phones Keith back and asks what his agenda was in the phone call. Brenda and Melissa chat and smoke dope in Brenda's house. Brenda confesses to masturbating her Shiatsu client, but can't really explain why she did it. Melissa suggests that it must be research for the novel Brenda is writing!

Claire arrives at Sarah's house. There's been a mix-up over the dates, because Sarah is expecting a large group of her hippy friends for a 'howl' weekend. Sarah is delighted that Claire has turned up, and promises her a fulfilling experience. Keith phones David and invites him out to dinner. Somewhat reluctantly, David agrees.

Claire meets Sarah's friends, who are all very bohemian. They remember Nathaniel being here, using a rolling machine to make spliffs. Ruth is angry when Nikolai cancels their plan for dinner, and remembering her solitary dinner the night before, invites Robbie to have dinner with her instead.

It's Jeffrey Shapiro's viewing, and the service is led by Rabbi Ari, who delivers a beautiful eulogy. Nate briefly imagines seeing a weeping Brenda, holding a baby, mourning in the congregation. Nate asks Rabbi Ari if he can ask her some questions about the Jewish method of mourning and death. He asks her if there's a particular way the Jewish faith tackles an imminent death. Ari replies that she just lives her life in a way that honours God. When Nate replies that he doesn't even know if God exists, Ari tells him it's probably time that he found out. Margaret is having a really hard time coping with the break-up of her marriage and rejects Brenda's efforts to comfort and support her.

Rico comes home to help his cousin Ramon with the rebuilding work, only to find Ramon having sex... but not with Vanessa, with another man! Rico is horrified and throws both of them out of his house. Ruth's meal with Robbie doesn't go particularly well. She finds his inane Plan-speak irritating, and finally tells him that she's had enough of talking in building metaphors. David waits and waits for Keith to turn up for their meal. Just as he is about to go home, he gets a call from Keith – Taylor has been taken into hospital for emergency surgery for appendicitis! All of her complaints over the past few weeks of a painful stomach weren't just excuses to avoid doing housework and finishing her meals. Keith spends the night by Taylor's bedside, and is pleasantly surprised the next morning when he wakes up and finds that David spent the night waiting in the hospital corridor.

Claire is smitten by Toby, one of the young men at Sarah's gathering. Together they look on in vague horror as the middle-aged men and women strip off and dance around a bonfire, shaking gourds.

Claire and Toby sneak off together and start to kiss. Toby tells her that he would never have sex with someone who he just met, which impresses her. They lie down together and fall asleep.

Nate goes to Jeffrey Shapiro's wake, where he continues to chat with Rabbi Ari. They briefly flirt around each other, but Ari is shocked when Nate tells her he hasn't told Brenda about his AVM yet. She tells him he has to tell her straight away. Brenda is driving around LA, not knowing what to do about her mother, when she begins to fantasise about having rough sex with strangers. At home later Nate makes love to Brenda, but unbeknownst to Nate, she seems quite unfulfilled by it, as if their safe love-making isn't enough for her any more.

As Claire prepares to head home, Toby asks for her phone number and Sarah gives her a cassette entitled 'Sarah Songs'. Rico has to swallow his pride and follow Ramon's lie when Ramon's wife Graciela comes to visit – he has to say that the reason Ramon isn't finishing the work on the house is because Rico wants to learn how to do it himself. Graciela clearly has no idea that her husband also likes men! When Claire gets home, Ruth doesn't ask her about her weekend away, but Claire is really surprised when she hears her mother singing along to a Joni Mitchell song on Sarah's cassette.

THE PRODIGAL SON

Now that Nate is preparing to marry Brenda, he spends quite some time evaluating exactly what getting married means. Although Nate is attracted to the beautiful young Rabbi Ari, he's far more interested in finding out her opinion about marriage and its place in current society. When Ari is amazed that Nate hasn't been honest with Brenda about his illness, Nate takes her views seriously – perhaps it's time that Nate was completely honest with his fiancée about every aspect of his life? Sadly for Nate, Brenda is being anything *but* honest with him. The closer she gets to the wedding, the more she seems to be rebelling against the prospect of marriage. When Margaret scoffs at Brenda's decision to marry Nate, it's an important moment – surely her mother, if anyone, must have a fairly good idea if this match will make her happy.

ANAL CONTROL FREAK

David must be deeply confused about his feelings for Keith. Not only did Keith push him away recently, but now – and immediately after breaking up with Eddie –he seems to want him back. Fearing that this reunion is just a case of love on the rebound, David tries to resist his automatic desire to get back together with Keith. When he does succumb to a dinner date, it looks as though Keith has messed him around yet again when he fails to turn up. However, Keith does have a legitimate excuse and David rushes to be by his side as Taylor undergoes emergency surgery. The fact that David is willing to stand by his man (or, more accurately, to sleep on some uncomfortable chairs a few feet away from him) proves to Keith that he has done the right thing in splitting up with Eddie. However, has David done the right thing by running back to Keith like a lovesick, obedient puppy?

MOMMY, DEAREST

Ruth is still trying to deal with her fear of loneliness. When she's left with nobody to have dinner with, she invites Robbie to join her. However, Ruth soon discovers that sometimes it's actually preferable to have silence and to keep your own company rather than listen to somebody you have no real connection with. When Ruth tells Robbie she's fed up 'talking in metaphors', she has finally realised that if she truly wants to rebuild her own life, she must do it on her own terms – not obeying the rules of some wacko programme. Later, Claire hears her mother singing along to a Joni Mitchell song – surely a sign of a *true* free spirit!

TEENAGE KICKS

Again trying to find out what her true purpose in life is, Claire goes against her mother's wishes and decides to spend the weekend with her Aunt Sarah. It's not quite the liberating experience that she expected – seeing Sarah's wacky hippy friends cavorting around half naked is a lot more intense than Claire had wanted! However, some good does come of the visit. Claire gets a lot closer to Sarah, and gains some valuable insights from her about Ruth and why she behaves in the way she does. Oh, and Claire goes home with a young man's phone number too…

DREAM ON, DREAMER

For once, it's Keith who dreams about getting back together with David – a reversal of the situation through most of the first season!

SOUNDTRACK

Antenna – '74 Willow' (Keith dreams of getting back together with David)

Nathan Larson and Nina Perrson – 'Just Because A Man' (Taylor watches MTV)

Nacho Sotomayor – 'Island God' (Brenda tells Margaret she's engaged)

Stoppa and Nobby – 'Sweet Lassi Dub' (Brenda tells Melissa that she 'crossed the line')

Timo Maas – 'Bad Days' (Nate meets Melissa)

Chopin – 'Opus 10 #3' (David and Rico run errands)

Los Zafiros – 'Bossa Cubana' (Rico discovers cousin Ramon in a compromising position)

Bellini – 'Que La Voce Sua Soave Vin Diletto' (from *I Puritani*) (Brenda visits Margaret)

Mercedes – 'It's Your Thing' (Brenda fantasises about a truck driver)

Joni Mitchell – 'Woodstock' (Aunt Sarah sings whilst cooking breakfast)

Joni Mitchell – 'Woodstock' (Ruth sings along, just as Sarah did previously)

SEX, DRUGS AND ROCK 'N' ROLL

The campfire naked dancing is probably something best left to those with a strong stomach or a very open mind! Brenda and Melissa share a couple of joints, but later Brenda can't seem to get in the slightest bit excited by the love-making she shares with Nate. Rico probably gets the biggest shock of everyone in this episode – half-expecting to come home and find his cousin Ramon having a fling with Vanessa, he actually discovers that Ramon sometimes bats for the other team too... Considering how uncomfortable Rico is with David's sexuality, this must really have been a tough one to swallow.

THE BRIGHT SIDE OF DEATH

Melissa: Please don't tell me you're one of those couples that likes to bicker in front of company until it gets uncomfortable and I have to leave and you guys fuck.
Nate and Brenda (together): No, no... (smiling uncomfortably)

ISN'T THAT WHATSHISNAME?

Sara Mornell (Jessica Shapiro) was a regular in the second series of *Judging Amy* as Carole Tobey. **Lee Garlington** (Fiona) played a blink-and-you'll-miss-her waitress in *Psycho II* (Richard Franklin, 1983) and *Psycho III* (Anthony Perkins, 1986) and Ronni the pet mortician in the *Friends* episode 'The One With The Boobies'. **Chris Ufland** (the unfortunate Jeffrey Shapiro) had small roles in *The Insider* (Michael Mann, 1999) and *Rules of Engagement* (William Friedkin, 2000). Fans of the late 70s highway patrol show *ChiPS* might recall **Robert Pine** (Basil), who played Sergeant Getraer. He's also had a recurring role in *The Bold and the Beautiful*. **Benjamin Banks** (Porno Guy 1) is better known as adult film star and director Steve St Croix. He and **Christi Lake** (Porno Girl) both starred in the video *The Palace of Pleasure* (Michael Santangelo, 1995).

UNANSWERED QUESTIONS

Are Toby's motives towards Claire truly honourable, or is he using her like her previous boyfriends have done?

EULOGY

Although 'Back to the Garden' moves a lot of the plotlines of the second season forward, it's not one of the most memorable. The performances and script are to their usual high standard, it's just that not a huge amount actually seems to happen and the story-lines seem to be treading water somewhat. There's still a great deal to admire, though, with the set pieces at Sarah's house providing some of the most enjoyable moments. And thankfully we finally get an explanation as to why Taylor has been moaning and whin-ing for so long! Hopefully having her appendix removed won't mean that her smart mouth has been taken out too...

EPISODE 21
IT'S THE MOST WONDERFUL TIME OF THE YEAR

Directed by: Alan Taylor
Written by: Scott Buck

GUEST CAST
Richard Jenkins as Nathaniel
Joanna Cassidy as Margaret
Jeremy Sisto as Billy
Ed O'Ross as Nikolai
Justina Machado as Vanessa
Aysia Polk as Taylor
Kellie Waymire as Melissa
Stark Sands as Toby
Ricardo Antonio Chavira as Ramon
Nicki Micheaux as Karla
Maria Carmen as Graciela

Rusty Schwimmer as Marilyn Johnson
Franc Ross as Jesse Johnson
W. Earl Brown as Pete
Tony Longo as Bitsy
Harley Zumbrum as Biker on Phone
Janet Wood as Saleswoman
Steve Gormley as Male Shopper
Brittany Lapham as Kid 1

Max Peters as Kid 2
Brooke Swift as Kid 3

WHO'S THE STIFF?

Jesse Ray Johnson, 1944-2001: Dressed as Father Christmas, Jesse waves at some nearby children and momentarily loses control of his motorbike, driving directly into the path of an oncoming lorry.

PLOT SUMMARY

It's December 23rd. Ruth is preparing her list of people who will be having Christmas dinner at the Fisher house. 'I wish I knew what I did to deserve such morose, surly children!' Of course, it's the anniversary of Nathaniel's death, which is why everyone is so jumpy. Rico finally tells Vanessa why he fired Ramon from fixing their house, and she's shocked.

David is delighted to welcome a biker funeral, as he seems to think that they all have Harley dealerships and are loaded. He's right – Jesse Johnson's widow Marilyn and her friends want a customised, spray-painted coffin and a Christmas Day funeral, and they will pay for the privilege.

David and Nate think back to the last time they saw their father alive. In Nate's case it was Thanksgiving (late November) 2000, when they shared quite a superficial yet loving conversation. David remembers dressing the Christmas tree with his father, but instead of stopping to talk, he went back down to the prep room to finish his work.

In a clothes store, Brenda flirts with a handsome man before grabbing his hand and rubbing it on her crotch. Just at that moment, the shop assistant tells the man his wife is ready to show him her new sweater, and then throws Brenda out. Ruth is having a similar but different problem with Nikolai – he wants her to take her knickers off and work in the shop without them on. Ruth is aghast at his saucy suggestion.

Brenda and Nate arrive at Margaret's new apartment for dinner. They realise that it's their first anniversary, and Nate presents her with his grandmother's engagement ring. Just then, Margaret reveals her 'special guest' for Christmas – it's Billy, who's been 'busted out' of hospital by Margaret. He's now living with his mother. Billy apologises to Nate for everything that happened. He says he was sick, and although he's still sick (and always will be), he can now manage it. Margaret lets slip that Brenda and Nate are engaged, and Billy seems genuinely pleased for them. However, Brenda is really upset that Billy has been taken out of hospital 'too early' and tells Nate she won't be Billy's nursemaid any longer.

David and Keith are trying to have a nice meal with Taylor, but her idea of a fun Christmas seems to be just watching *The Simpsons*. Keith's also having trouble dealing with the recent shooting. On their way to church on Christmas Eve, Ruth and Claire stop off at Nikolai's shop, only to find him lying on the floor, the shop wrecked. His legs have been broken and he will have to stay off them for eight weeks, so it is decided that he will stay at the Fishers'.

It's Jesse's Christmas Day memorial service. The bikers are happy, the beer is flowing and the tributes are paid. Then they play Jesse's favourite song – 'Born To Be Wild'. As Claire brings Toby to the house, she remembers her last conversation with Nathaniel, when Gabe phoned her up and invited her to the crystal meth party. As the Fishers sit down to their meal, the biker funeral carries on at full volume downstairs. Then Keith and Taylor show up as surprise guests. Ruth asks Keith to say grace, and he's so eloquent that David's last doubts about getting back together melt away. During the meal, Brenda and Claire have a heart-to-heart in the kitchen whilst knocking back red wine. Claire reveals that she's been talking with Billy via email for the past few months, which shocks Brenda. Complaining of a headache, Brenda heads home whilst Nate keeps an eye on the bikers.

Rico remembers his last meeting with Nathaniel, when 'Mr F' gave him the day off. Just then, Ramon bursts in and punches Rico to the floor. Vanessa has told Graciela what happened, and Graciela has taken the children away from him. Rico is incandescent with anger at both Vanessa and Ramon the 'fucking homo'. As the biker funeral is still progressing, Nate agrees to stay to supervise whilst David goes home with Keith and Taylor. Claire and Toby's relationship goes into a nosedive. 'When you take a look at your life, there's not much to be angry at,' points out the smug and supercilious Toby. They realise that there is nothing to keep them together, and Toby leaves. Claire then goes upstairs and chats online with Billy, sharing their Christmas Day horror stories with each other.

Marilyn has a chat with Nate and she says how much she loved Jesse. She's glad he lived the way he did – if he was more careful, he might have lived longer, but she probably wouldn't have enjoyed being with him as much. Nate tells her that he used to have a motorbike but doesn't ride any more. They both agree that the philosophy of living each day as if it was your last is a good one.

Ruth's memory of her last meeting with Nathaniel makes her cry. Arriving back at home, Keith is surprised when Karla shows up with presents for everyone. Taylor is delighted to see her mother.

Brenda tells Nate about Billy's emails to Claire and it spirals into a huge argument between the two of them, Brenda upset that Billy no longer confides in her, Nate terrified about Claire forming a connection with the unstable Billy. Nate and Brenda make up with violent, passionate sex, which suddenly goes wrong when Nate has another seizure. He is finally forced to tell Brenda about his AVM. 'Don't worry – I won't let anything happen to you,' she promises, as she cradles his head in her lap. The next morning, Nate discovers that Marilyn has left him Jesse's Harley-Davidson, and Nate takes to the coast road for a high-speed drive – living every day as if it were his last.

THE PRODIGAL SON

One of the really useful things about working as a funeral director must be the handy supply of advice from the recently bereaved. Certainly that is true for Nate when Marilyn Johnson tells him to live for the moment and fill every day with experiences. Not only does this inspire him to take up riding a motorbike again (thanks largely to the very generous present from Marilyn!) but it also enables him to finally tell Brenda about his medical condition. When every day *could* very possibly be his last, what is the point in hiding away and denying that there's a problem? By facing the matter head-on, Nate finds a way to bond still further with Brenda. For Brenda, the news is, in some ways, everything she could have wished for. Having lost one person to nurse, she all of a sudden finds another one. Part of her is delighted to be back on safe territory, while the other part of her wants to run away screaming...

MOMMY, DEAREST

More than anything else, Ruth just wants to have a nice family Christmas. This, of course, is not going to happen. First of all, when it comes to the Fishers, there's no such thing as 'normal' – they all bring so many issues to the dining table there's no chance of avoiding chilly stares or awkward silences over the cranberry sauce. Secondly, Nikolai is badly assaulted and left with his legs smashed. And most importantly, Christmas is the first anniversary of the death of Nathaniel. No matter how much Ruth would like to paper over the cracks and pretend that everything is fine and dandy, the pain and suffering of the past year will always come to the surface. What Ruth finds difficult to comprehend is that acknowledging everybody's feelings would be the best way to commemorate Nathaniel's passing.

TEENAGE KICKS

Claire faces problems in this episode from the two men in her life – her potential new boyfriend Toby, and the man she's secretly been emailing and chatting to for the past six months, Billy Chenowith. The two men behave in completely different ways to each other. Toby suggests to Claire that she's actually got life pretty easy, thereby completely negating what she's going through (especially on the anniversary of her father's death). On the other hand, Billy is there as a confidant for her, listening to her problems and empathising with the trauma of family life. It's really not at all surprising that Claire dumps Toby and spends most of Christmas night chatting online to Billy. Claire is certainly maintaining her habit of being attracted to the dangerous or 'unsafe' type of man!

DREAM ON, DREAMER

All of the main cast get a flashback to the final time they saw Nathaniel before his untimely death. They are all poignant, emotional and astoundingly well shot. Sublime stuff.

SOUNDTRACK

Andy Williams – 'Let It Snow' (The Fishers discuss their plans for Christmas)

The Mighty Turbans – 'Jingle Bells' (Claire and Toby at the mall)

Joel Evans – 'What Child Is This' (Brenda molests a male shopper)

Mozart – Allegro Concerto For Flute And Orchestra In D Major (The flower shop)

Dodie Stevens – 'Merry Christmas Baby' (David remembers Nathaniel)

Bobby Timmons – 'Deck The Halls' (It's Billy!)

Scott Hamilton – 'Have Yourself A Merry Little Christmas' (Brenda tells Billy she's engaged)

The Allman Brothers – 'Midnight Rider' (Jesse's eulogy)

Steppenwolf – 'Born To Be Wild' (Jesse's favourite song)

The Outlaws – 'Green Grass And High Tides' (Brenda arrives for Christmas dinner)

Mozart – 'Allegro Divertimento In D Major For Strings' (The Fishers' Christmas dinner)

Bach – 'Sinfonia In G (Christmas Oratorio)' (Christmas dinner)

Lynyrd Skynyrd – 'Free Bird' (Claire tells Brenda that she's been emailing Billy)

Blue Öyster Cult – 'Don't Fear The Reaper' (Bikers salute Jesse)

Lynyrd Skynyrd – 'Sweet Home Alabama' (Toby and Claire split up)

Blue Öyster Cult – 'Don't Fear The Reaper' (Nate hits the road)

SEX, DRUGS AND ROCK 'N' ROLL

Brenda yet again goes 'over the line' when she almost has sex in the middle of a department store with an unwitting man who just happens to be shopping there. Bad girl!

THE BRIGHT SIDE OF DEATH

Marilyn: No flirting with the faggoty elves!
Jesse: Can I help it if the elves think I'm a stud?

Shop assistant: Can I help you?
Brenda: Yes, I'm looking for clothes so expensive only an idiot would buy them. Oh, there they are...

ISN'T THAT WHATSHISNAME?

A regular in the TV series *The Guardian* and *Picket Fences*, **Rusty Schwimmer** (Marilyn Johnson) has also popped up in the films *Candyman* (Bernard Rose, 1992), *A Little Princess* (Alfonso Cuaron, 1995), *Twister* (Jan De Bont, 1996), *Amistad* (Steven Spielberg, 1999), *EdTV* (Ron Howard, 1999) and *The Perfect Storm* (Wolfgang Petersen, 2000).

UNANSWERED QUESTIONS

✟ What happened to Nikolai's legs? Who smashed up the flower shop?
✟ Is Billy really healthy again? Should Margaret have signed his release papers, or was she just feeling lonely?

EULOGY

After the slightly lacklustre previous episode, we're back on form again with this riveting examination of the rules, regulations and customs of the annual family Christmas gathering. Of the two parties we see in detail – one at Margaret Chenowith's, then the one at the Fisher house – it's hard to decide which is the least messed up. Margaret seems to have discharged her son from a secure mental health ward just so she isn't lonely at Christmas, whereas Ruth issues the usual Christmas ultimatum that everyone is going to be together and everyone is going to be happy, whether they like it or not. Even the Diaz family don't escape, when Vanessa accidentally lets slip about Ramon's bisexuality. It doesn't look like many of the *Six Feet Under* characters would agree that Christmas is the most wonderful time of the year! In fact, only Nate and Brenda seem to have a positive resolution to the festive period, and even that is clouded by the possibility of their happiness being snatched away at any moment. How terribly festive!

EPISODE 22
SOMEONE ELSE'S EYES

Directed by: Michael Cuesta
Written by: Alan Ball

GUEST CAST
Richard Jenkins as Nathaniel
Jeremy Sisto as Billy
Lily Taylor as Lisa
Ed O'Ross as Nikolai
Kellie Waymire as Melissa
Aysia Polk as Taylor
Joel Brooks as Robbie
Tim Maculan as Father Jack
Nicki Micheaux as Karla
Ilia Volok as Yuri

Dina Meyer as The Widow
Leeza Gibbons as Herself
Ashley Gardner as Daughter 1
Stephanie Erb as Daughter 2
Timothy V. Murphy as Louis Winchell
Joe Nieves as Construction Worker 1
Chris Ellis as Construction Worker 2

WHO'S THE STIFF?

Dwight Edgar Garrison, 1945-2002: Head smashed open by a metal lunchbox that was accidentally dropped by a construction worker.

PLOT SUMMARY

Brenda takes Nate to a cliff-top overlooking the Pacific Ocean, the location where she wants to have their marriage ceremony. Nate worries that Brenda is marrying him out of sympathy, but she promises him that she's marrying him for the 'here and now' – however long Nate lives for. However, she objects to having a rabbi or any other religious person officiating at the ceremony.

Keith is having difficulty sleeping now that Karla has taken Taylor back. He goes round to see his sister and is livid when he realises that she is taking drugs again. Keith gives her an ultimatum – either check into a rehab course or he will have her arrested. Karla agrees to the rehab course.

Ruth asks Claire to keep an eye on Nikolai whilst she's at work but Claire is reluctant, not seeing it as her responsibility. Nikolai's housebound status is now starting to become wearing for all the family – except Ruth, who sees it as the 'next stage' of their relationship. Rico even ends up being emotionally blackmailed by Nikolai into sharing his lunch with him to keep the chair-ridden Russian company.

Dwight Garrison's widow gets a shock when she finds out that he made an arrangement to be buried with his late *first* wife, not with her. His children are delighted, as they never liked their stepmother. The problem escalates until they have a stand-up argument over where Dwight is to be buried. Nate bellows at them to have more respect and points out that it's not their decision – Dwight left instructions on where he wanted to be buried.

Billy visits Brenda whilst Margaret is away on a cruise for the 'recently separated'. When Brenda tells Billy about Nate's illness, he says he now realises why she's marrying him. Billy then says that her protective behaviour towards him actually contributed to his illness – 'Our relationship is really toxic' – and that they should 'disengage' from each other for a period so that he can continue his healing.

Nate catches Claire going out to meet Billy and warns her to be careful. Ruth tells Nikolai that she's been going through his book-keeping system and it's in a terrible state. She warns him that he could be in trouble if he gets audited, but Nikolai tells Ruth to keep her nose out of his private business.

Out shopping, Nate is stunned to bump into Lisa, his 'fuck buddy' from Seattle. She tells him that she's actually been living in Los Angeles for a few months. He's even more stunned when Lisa reveals she's five months pregnant, and that he's the father. She's unwilling to let him have anything to do with her or the baby, convinced that he's a heartless bastard who abandoned her.

Brenda goes to a live reading by author Louis Winchell of his book *The Lie of Romance*, and the words seem to ring painfully true for her. In fact, she's so taken by his words that she ends up having sex with him in a toilet. Like all of her recent excessive behaviour, this is typed up for the book she is working on. Brenda later describes her experience to Melissa – she tells her it was 'such a fucking rush', and seems completely revitalised and energised by it. She briefly contemplates that she may be losing her mind, but rejects Melissa's suggestion that she should talk to a therapist.

Billy invites Claire to take part in his latest project – she agrees, but is somewhat surprised when the project turns out to be taking photos of him naked. Claire leaves when the experience proves to be a bit too intense for Billy and he starts to lose emotional control.

Ruth gets a frightening visit from a guy called Yuri who is trying to track down Nikolai. He's clearly involved in some way with the beating Nikolai received. Nikolai confesses to Ruth that he owes money to the men who helped him set up his business.

Keith is having real difficulty dealing with all his problems – Taylor, Karla, the shooting – and shouts at David. David says he's happy to be there for Keith so that he has someone to unburden his problems on. Keith later suggests to David that he should move in. Unknown to Keith, Karla is taking blood samples from Taylor and passing them off as her own for the drug tests that her rehab course makes her take.

Father Jack conducts Dwight's memorial service. Mrs Garrison is very grateful to the Fishers and thanks them for their help. She is deeply upset that she only had six years with her husband, but Nate points out that six years is more than a lot of people get.

Billy emails Claire some copies of the pictures she took. Despite being scared by his earlier meltdown, the pictures seem to intrigue her.

THE PRODIGAL SON

Yet another twist in the saga of Nate and Brenda, as a third (and by extension, fourth) person enters into their tangled romantic equation. Nate discovers that he's about to become a father – the night of 'comfort' he shared with Lisa has had far-reaching consequences. Of course, any normal person would try to find some way of breaking the news to their partner, but the old Fisher curse of secret-keeping comes into play yet again and Nate decides to keep it from Brenda for now. Naturally enough, Brenda has her own little secret too – she's cheated on Nate with a complete stranger (and an author to boot!) The most worrying thing for the future of Nate and Brenda's relationship is just how excited and revitalised she seems after the anonymous sex. If she feels *this* good, won't she do the same kind of thing again?

ANAL CONTROL FREAK

Keith seems to have too many problems to deal with on his own. He is still worried over the shooting and is scared for both his junkie sister Karla and his niece Taylor. The one person Keith should be relying upon is David, but instead of sharing his pain and fears, he just keeps lashing out at him. Despite this lack of communication, David behaves impeccably, understanding Keith's stressful situation and allowing Keith to verbally hit out at him. Considering the amount of abuse David takes, it must come as a fantastic surprise when Keith asks him to move in. Perhaps, after all he's been through, Keith is realising that he really does need David around him if he's going to be able to deal with his problems.

MOMMY, DEAREST

With Nikolai at home all the time, Ruth is back in her element – finally she has somebody to mother again! The rest of her family don't appreciate having a fully grown baby brought into their house, though, and Nikolai certainly doesn't like it when Ruth starts poking around in the finances of the flower shop. But Ruth is so wrapped up in her own little world of being able to control things again that she doesn't even notice.

TEENAGE KICKS

Claire's involvement with Billy was always liable to be 'interesting', so when she agrees to help him with his new project she knows that it's likely to be something far from the norm. Bearing in mind Nate's warnings about Billy's unpredictability, Claire has the presence of mind to remove herself from any possible danger when he starts to find the whole experience overwhelming. When Claire sees the photographs, her eyes are opened to a new possibility: the photos are superb works of art, displaying her true talent. Claire's mind begins to see a possible future path…

SOUNDTRACK

Nelly Furtado – 'Shit On The Radio' (Taylor watches TV as Keith arrives)

Biber – 'Sonata Problaba' (Flower shop)

Four Tet – 'Glue Of The World' (Billy decides to spend time away from Brenda)

Blue Six – 'Pure (Jay's Nightlife Mix)' (Billy and Claire chat)

Eels – 'Souljacker (Part 1)' (Brenda starts to lose it and rips up phone numbers)

De Wolfe Orchestra – 'Heading Home' (muzak) (Nate bumps into Lisa)

Orchestral Archives – 'Fare Thee Well' (muzak) (Lisa tells Nate he's going to be a dad)

Grieg – 'The Death Of Ase' (Yuri leaves a message for Nikolai)
Kings Of Convenience – 'I Don't Know What I Can Save You From (Royksopp Mix)' (Nate visits Brenda but they are both keeping secrets)
Handel – *Xerxes* (Dwight Garrison's funeral)

SEX, DRUGS AND ROCK 'N' ROLL

Brenda's casual shag with the author marks a new line that she's crossed. Previously she's fantasised about having anonymous sex, but this is the first time that she's acted on those impulses. It won't be the last. Keith finally gets Karla to admit that she's back on drugs and manages to persuade her into going into rehab. Unfortunately, Keith hasn't counted on the deviousness of the typical addict in hiding their habit…

ISN'T THAT WHATSHISNAME?

Dina Meyer (The Widow) starred in *Starship Troopers* (Paul Verhoeven, 1997) and plays former Batgirl Barbara Gordon on the TV show *Birds of Prey*. **Leeza Gibbons** is an American TV presenter and talk-show host.

UNANSWERED QUESTIONS

✟ Will Karla be able to keep her ongoing habit secret?
✟ When is Nate going to tell Brenda about his impending fatherhood?
✟ When is Brenda going to tell Nate about her infidelity?
✟ How much money does Nikolai actually owe Yuri?

EULOGY

In this episode we start the long descent into real darkness. Previously in *Six Feet Under* there have always been the occasional light-hearted episodes to break up the melancholy, but from this point on there's not much to laugh about. That's hardly surprising considering the stresses and strains that are being placed upon the lives of our favourite characters – infidelity, loan sharks, mental illness, drug addiction, loneliness, lack of direction, new parenthood, looking after a child, fear for loved ones... it's all there. Unlike most lesser 'drama series' (read: soap operas), none of these issues appear forced or clumsily handled. As every new layer of pain and suffering is applied to the Fishers and their friends, it all appears perfectly natural, logical and believable – which demonstrates the quality of the writing, acting and direction of the whole series.

EPISODE 23
THE SECRET

Directed by: Alan Poul
Written by: Bruce Eric Kaplan

GUEST CAST
Lili Taylor as Lisa
Joanna Cassidy as Margaret
Robert Foxworth as Bernard
Ed O'Ross as Nikolai
Kellie Waymire as Melissa
Aysia Polk as Taylor
Marina Black as Parker
Nicki Micheaux as Karla
Giancarlo Rodriguez as Julio Diaz

James Morrison as Swinger Husband (Ted)
Kim Myers as Dr Michaelson
Victor McCay as Claire's Teacher
Ben Lin as Benjamin Srisai
June Kyoko Lu as Bette Srisai
Art Chudabala as Phil Srisai
Beverly Leech as Swinger Wife
Scott Hoxby as Male Coke User
Anita Finlay as Female Coke User
Shawn Huang as Thai Boy
Jenna Boyd as Seven-Year-Old Girl

Paul Butcher as Five-Year-Old Boy
Gretchen Storms as Teenager

WHO'S THE STIFF?

Benjamin Srisai 1935-2002: Suffers a heart attack whilst taking the rubbish out for recycling.

PLOT SUMMARY

Claire continues her new hobby by photographing the corpses in Fisher & Sons. Claire's friend Parker is really supportive of her new skill, and then drops the bombshell that following her cheating scam, she's been accepted into Yale. Claire didn't get the grades for UCLA, and is now unsure what to do with her life. Lisa arrives to get Nate to sign a form giving up custodial rights for the baby. She admits she would have preferred to have the baby with somebody who wanted to be a father, but says everything's going to be OK.

David starts to move some of his furniture into Keith's apartment, but begins to feel as if he's compromising too much in their relationship. When he tries to tell Keith that he feels as though he can never complain or do anything wrong in case it jeopardises their relationship, Keith refuses to talk about it. David finally realises that some of the problems they had in their relationship last time may not have been entirely due to him still being in the closet.

Nikolai takes his leg casts off a week early and decides to move back home, concerning Ruth greatly. She decides to visit him, and takes a few things with her for a 'surprise sleepover' that consists of cleaning and 'prettifying' his house. However, Ruth finally snaps and asks Nikolai why he doesn't just move in with her. He says that he loves her, but he just doesn't want to move in with anybody, that maybe he's 'not capable of it'. Disappointed, Ruth goes home.

Phil and Bette Srisai arrive for the induction meeting. David's knowledge of Buddhist funeral services impresses them greatly.

Brenda goes to see the therapist Melissa recommended. She confesses that she's had sex with strangers, and thinks it's strange behaviour. She doesn't feel guilty about it, but wants the therapist to help her not 'feel edgy' about what she's doing in relation to Nate. She says she thinks it may even be healthy for her to have a part of her life that has nothing to do with Nate.

Later, Brenda and Nate visit Margaret to plan Brenda's forthcoming bridal shower. They are shocked to discover that Bernard is back – after begging for forgiveness – and Mr and Mrs Chenowith seem ecstatic about their reunion. Brenda is disgusted at her mother's lack of backbone, but Margaret warns Brenda not to let her own issues about commitment ruin her relationship with Nate.

Owing to Rico having to complete a restoration and Vanessa being away, Nate has to look after young Julio for a few hours and the pair seem to bond very well indeed. Claire is disappointed when her teacher fails her English paper – even though it consists of her photographs of the Fisher & Sons corpses. She's forced to actually write something in order to be able to graduate and go to college.

Brenda suggests to Melissa that she should include Nate in her next 'moment of madness' by going to a swingers' party. Melissa knows somebody who organises such parties, so Brenda asks if she can go with her to the next one. She phones Nate to tell him she's not feeling well; he tells her to stay in bed and look after herself. Brenda is of course going to the sex party, where she snorts cocaine, gets drunk and indulges in a threesome with a married couple.

When Claire shows Nate her portfolio, he is furious at the potential lawsuits she could have caused by taking photos of the Fisher & Sons clients without their families' permission. Claire later goes to see East Valley College with Parker and is disappointed by the facilities and the prospect of spending time there.

On her way to Saturday lunch with Keith and David, Karla accidentally knocks over a homeless man, but instead of stopping to help, she drives off. Taylor begs her mother to tell the cops, but Karla doesn't want to because they'll take Taylor away. Taylor confides in David about the homeless man, but then, realising her mistake, laughs and says it was just a joke. Later, David tells Keith about Taylor's bizarre story. Keith phones his precinct and discovers that a homeless man was indeed killed by a car matching Karla's.

Brenda shows up an hour late for her own bridal shower party. She's hungover and wired, and tells Ruth exactly what she was up to last night with the married couple. Not knowing if she's joking or not, Ruth confesses that she loves Brenda for her free spirit, for the inability to smother people and lose them. She admits that's why she initially hated Brenda, but that's why she now loves her. Ruth then has a conversation with Claire, who admits that she's tired and scared and fed up with dealing with life and the lies and petty concerns forced upon her by society. Ruth stops the conversation to go to the bathroom, where she bumps into Bernard Chenowith for the first time. Ruth is shocked when Bernard asks her what help she's getting for her clearly depressed daughter, but she won't talk about it.

Karla is arrested by the police and taken away, leaving Taylor to be looked after by Keith and David. Brenda, who feels as though she's starting to lose control over her life, tells Melissa to leave her alone, saying that she needs to be around people with stronger values, and that she possibly wouldn't have started to do all of the messed-up stuff if Melissa hadn't been around. Melissa says that if she needs to sublimate her own issues then that's fine, but that there is no point ever trying to rebuild their friendship.

Nate meets with Lisa and tells her that he really needs to be a part of their child's life. When he admits that Brenda doesn't even know about Lisa and the baby yet, Lisa is furious with him. 'If you can't put anyone but yourself first, how can you possibly be a father?' She walks away, telling Nate to leave her and her child alone.

THE PRODIGAL SON

Nate gets to spend some time with Rico's son Julio and it's an eye-opening experience for him. Realising that he has a child of his own on the way, and seeing what joy a child can bring to its parents' lives, Nate decides to take that responsibility on board. He's shocked when Lisa tells him to get lost, but she's absolutely right – until Nate can bring himself to admit his mistakes and put other people first, he's not ready to become a father.

ANAL CONTROL FREAK

David comes to an important understanding in this episode. For over a year now, David has always believed that the reason for the break-up of his relationship with Keith was because he had yet to come to terms with his own sexuality. He's now realised that some of the reasons for their break-up might have had something to do with Keith's own controlling nature. Keith needs things to go his own way for him to be happy, and when things don't, he rebels and fights back – a bit like a baby throwing its toys out of the pram. Although their argument stems from inappropriate furniture, David realises that Keith is actually having a real problem coping with sharing his life with anyone. When Keith is forced to turn his own sister in to the authorities, David realises that his behaviour is almost certainly going to continue to deteriorate.

MOMMY, DEAREST

Ruth begins to realise the consequences of her 'smother love' in this episode. Nikolai refuses to move in with her, and it even looks as though her control-freak behaviour may spell the end for the relationship entirely. When Ruth shares a quiet moment's conversation with Brenda and explains how much she admires the young woman's ability to let people breathe, it's a lovely moment of self-awareness for Ruth. But is it too late for her to change?

TEENAGE KICKS

Claire is beginning to face the reality of life after school, and it's a worrying prospect. Having failed the exams to get into UCLA, and realising that her best friend Parker will soon be leaving for Yale, she's forced to examine her life closely and make some important decisions. Sadly, those answers are not yet forthcoming, even though all the pieces of the jigsaw are already there for her to put into place. Right now, she's just too upset and depressed by the whole concept to see the wood for the trees.

DREAM ON, DREAMER

Nate has a very unsettling dream about the children he could have been responsible for parenting – the children who were aborted, miscarried or stillborn.

SOUNDTRACK

Caetano Veloso – 'Onde O Rio E Mais Baino' (Dinner at Margaret's)

Caetano Veloso – 'Minha Voz, Minha Vida' (Margaret gives Brenda some advice)

Frou Frou – 'Breathe In' (Brenda agrees to go with Melissa to her party)

Caroline Lavelle – 'All I Have (Kid Loco Mix)' (Keith and David argue)

Steely Dan – 'Hey 19'/Soul II Soul – 'Keep On Movin' (Teddy Riley's Rubba Dubba)'/Jazzanova – 'Bohemian Sunset'/Bryan Ferry – 'Kiss And Tell'/Marvin Gaye – 'After The Dance' (Swingers' party)

Traditional Thai Music – 'Hun Graboug'/Music From Thailand and Laos – 'Daw Thong' (Benjamin's funeral)

Dave Brubeck – 'Broadway Bossa Nova'/'Upstage Rhumba' (Bridal shower)

SEX, DRUGS AND ROCK 'N' ROLL

Brenda's night at the swingers' party contains practically every vice known to man. Like any good researcher trying to find out facts for a book, Brenda decides to immerse herself fully in the topic, and ends up taking cocaine and taking part in a threesome with a not especially attractive couple. Nice.

THE BRIGHT SIDE OF DEATH

Nikolai: Ruthie – why do I want little cherries in my drawers?
Ruth: It's hard to explain. You just do.

ISN'T THAT WHATSHISNAME?

James Morrison (Swinger Husband) played Lt Col 'TC' McQueen in the TV series *Space: Above and Beyond*. **Kim Myers** (Dr Michaelson) made her film debut in *A Nightmare on Elm Street Part 2: Freddy's Revenge* (Jack Sholder, 1985). **Victor McCay** (Claire's Teacher) has appeared in a number of episodes of *The West Wing*.

EULOGY

Watching Brenda's slide into further degradation is becoming increasingly unsettling to watch. Brenda knows that what she is doing is wrong, but tries to convince herself (and the therapist she visits) that she is sophisticated enough to rise above the morals that ordinary mortals live by. We know that Brenda is a massively intelligent woman, who is so aware of her own personality and character that she should be able to see the way out of the maze she finds herself trapped in. Unfortunately, there's still a lot further for Brenda to fall before she can begin to try and climb back up again. If Brenda were single or if she were in a relationship where both partners had decided it was non-exclusive, then there might be some justification... but even Brenda can't come up with a rational explanation for what she's doing.

EPISODE 24
THE LIAR & THE WHORE

Directed by: Miguel Arteta
Written by: Rick Cleveland

GUEST CAST
Glenn Fitzgerald as Aaron Buchbinder
Molly Parker as Rabbi Ari
Harriet Sansom Harris as Catherine Collins
Ed O'Ross as Nikolai
Justina Machado as Vanessa
Julie White as Mitzi Dalton Huntley
Joel Brooks as Robbie
Aysia Polk as Taylor
Marina Black as Parker
Nicki Micheaux as Karla
David Norona as Gary Deitman
Ilia Volok as Yuri
Jessica D. Stone as Young Brenda
Beverly Todd as Lucille Charles

James Pickens Jr as Mr Charles
Kim Coles as Dolores
Lynda Scarlino as Edith Kirky
Wilda Taylor as Ramona Kippleman
Peter Birkenhead as David's Lawyer
Bruce Wright as Detective

Michael Childers as Coroner
Austin Nichols as Tall Stoner
Chase Penny as Short Stoner
Anthony Sherritt as Summons Server
Amy Wieczorek as Party Guest
Thomas Garner as Party Guest

WHO'S THE STIFF?

Edith Kirky, 1929 – 2002: Dies in the nursing home where Vanessa Diaz works, after complaining about being in extreme pain.

PLOT SUMMARY

Taylor is having a hard time dealing with losing her mother yet again. Similarly, Keith worries about the imminent arrival of his father, who is due to visit. Nate gets served with a summons from Mrs Collins, the wife of the man who fell overboard in 'In Place of Anger'. After demanding to see her husband's corpse, she's now suing Fisher & Sons for $500,000 of emotional damage.

Taylor has got some magic mushrooms ('shrooms') and tells Claire to keep tomorrow free so they can trip together. Meanwhile, Nate and Brenda attend their first pre-marriage counselling session with Rabbi Ari. Afterwards, Nate confesses to Brenda about sleeping with Lisa on his trip to Seattle and the fact that Lisa's now expecting his baby. Brenda doesn't know how to respond, and walks away. She later tries to get in touch with Billy, desperate to speak to him about her problems.

David is horrified to discover that the lawsuit seems practically watertight; his lawyer advises him to settle with Mrs Collins with as much money as they can afford. Ruth goes to see Claire's counsellor Gary Deitman, who reassures her that Claire isn't depressed – but that he thinks Ruth might be!

Keith is angry when his parents ask to take Taylor back to San Diego to live with them.

Rabbi Ari calls over to give Nate some details of a possible funeral, but when she notices how depressed Nate seems, she talks to him about his problems. Ari tells Nate to give Brenda some time to cope with the shocking news.

As Rico starts work on the body of Edith Kirky, he notices lots of bruising around her throat and a large hotdog stuck in her windpipe. Rico is convinced that something like that couldn't have happened accidentally, despite the fact that the post-mortem suggested heart failure. A coroner gets called in, and is as surprised as Rico by the initial idea of what the cause of death was. Their suspicions are raised still further when they discover that Vanessa was one of the people who tried to resuscitate Edith.

Nate goes to see Rabbi Ari's friend, Aaron Buchbinder, who is dying of pancreatic cancer and needs to arrange his funeral. He's quite negative about life in general – he should already be dead, having survived six months longer than his life expectancy.

Yuri comes into the shop, hoping to speak to Nikolai. Ruth tells him that Nikolai isn't there, and asks how much is owed. Having already been to the bank and withdrawn the money, she hands over $87,000 to Yuri. When Nikolai finds out about the payment, he is furious at Ruth for intruding on his business. Even Robbie won't allow Ruth to get away with interfering in Nikolai's life without commenting on her tendency towards co-dependent behaviour.

Mitzi comes over to the Fishers and tells them that Kroehner is behind Mrs Collins' legal fight. She offers one last time to buy them out at a significantly reduced amount. David and Nate ask Ruth to borrow the remains of Nathaniel's life insurance to pay off Mrs Collins, but it's too late – all of the money has gone to pay off Nikolai's debt. David meets with Mrs Collins and accuses her of using the lawsuit to try and reclaim the years of abuse she suffered at the hands of her husband. On the verge of tears, Mrs Collins rips up the summons document.

Claire and Taylor, high on the shrooms, decide to use Claire's sewing machine to make some clothes. Claire makes her mother a pair of trousers, and in her heightened state tells Ruth how much she loves her.

Meanwhile, Brenda is smoking a joint on her veranda. Two young men come along and ask for a joint. She takes her blouse off and gets them to follow her inside. They have sex with Brenda, who during the act imagines seeing herself as a child looking back at her.

Vanessa is kept waiting all night by the police before they interrogate her about the death of Edith. The police seem to think that the old lady in the next bed, Ramona, was responsible for killing her roommate. The nursing home needs to find a scapegoat for the death, though, so both Vanessa and her colleague Dolores get the sack.

The next morning, Claire is horrified by the trousers she made for her mother, but Ruth gives her an application form for an art college. Keith finally stands up to his bully of a father and says that Taylor will be staying with him and David for the foreseeable future.

Brenda finally comes round to see Nate. She tells Nate that she 'can't lose' him. 'As fucked up as you are, you are the sanest thing in my life.' Brenda tells Nate that she loves him and they hug.

THE PRODIGAL SON

Finally, Nate manages to sum up the courage to admit his infidelity to Brenda. However, she is not as truthful as he is. Instead of taking the opportunity to own up and admit her mistakes, Brenda opts to walk away and let Nate believe that he is the only one to have put their relationship in jeopardy. Nothing seems to go right for poor Nate, though – an earlier moment of kindness towards Mrs Collins almost leads to the ruin of Fisher & Sons. It's only due to the quick thinking and risk-taking of David that the business is saved. About the only thing that Nate seems to do right is his visit to see Aaron Buchbinder. Nate sees a lot of himself in the young man – someone dying before their time who's angry with the hand that life has dealt him. Nate's decision to be with Aaron to the very end is a noble and thoughtful act that shows a great deal more maturity than most of his earlier decisions. Perhaps, as Nate deals with impending fatherhood and the accompanying responsibilities, he is finally starting to grow up.

MOMMY, DEAREST

Ruth's decision to pay off Nikolai's debt is a rather clumsy attempt to maintain her relationship. Sensing that Nikolai was on the verge of breaking up with her, Ruth resorts to trying to buy his love – and although Nikolai is clearly grateful for getting the loathsome Yuri off his back, he genuinely isn't happy at now being in emotional and moral debt to somebody else.

DREAM ON, DREAMER

During their first counselling session with Rabbi Ari, Brenda and Nate imagine that they are wearing appropriate T-shirts: 'Liar' for Nate and 'Whore' for Brenda.

Brenda smokes a bong of dope and has a flashback to a sex party her parents had when she was a little girl.

SOUNDTRACK

The Doves – 'Meet Me At The Pier' (Claire discovers that Sarah has given her magic mushrooms)

Mendelssohn – 'String Quartet, Opus 44 #1' (Nikoli and Ruth are visted by Yuri)

Laura Nyro – 'Poverty Train' (Brenda remembers one of her parents' parties)

Tosca – 'Orozsco (Dubphonic Mix)' (Brenda seduces the two teenagers)

Air – 'The Way You Look Tonight' (Claire and Parker get creative!)

Mozart – 'Quartet In D Major' (Nikolai tells Ruth off for helping him)

SEX, DRUGS AND ROCK 'N' ROLL

Claire and Taylor enjoy an evening on magic mushrooms, and get all creative with a sewing machine as a result. Brenda, meanwhile, smokes dope and has sex with two young men.

THE BRIGHT SIDE OF DEATH

Ruth: Claire, are you depressed?
Claire: I'm not going to even answer that.
Ruth: Well, whatever you're going through, I hope you're not going to blame me.

ISN'T THAT WHATSHISNAME?

Glenn Fitzgerald (Aaron Buchbinder) starred in the satirical movie send-up of reality TV shows, *Series 7: The Contenders* (Daniel Minahan, 2001). **Harriet Sansom Harris** (Catherine Collins) plays the chain-smoking agent Bebe Glazer of *Frasier*. **James Pickens Jr** (Mr Charles) has been a recurring guest star on *Roseanne* (Chuck Mitchell), *Another World* (Zack Edwards), *The Practice* (Det. Mike McKrew) and *The X-Files* (FBI Deputy Director Alvin Kersh). **Kim Coles** (Dolores) is a well-known celebrity face in the USA – she was a member of the *In Living Color* team and is a regular panellist on shows like *Hollywood Squares* and *To Tell the Truth*.

UNANSWERED QUESTIONS

✟ Has Ruth been able to buy Nikolai's love?
✟ Will Brenda ever have enough research material for her book?
✟ Has Claire finally discovered her vocation in life?

EULOGY

Whilst attending their first pre-wedding counselling session with Rabbi Ari, both Nate and Brenda have a realisation of what they both are – a liar and a whore. The funny thing is that each label could be applied to either one of them. Away from the car crash of a relationship that is Brenda and Nate, the poor Diaz family are having to cope with a particularly unfair chain of circumstances as Vanessa is fired because of Rico's diligence. The dark clouds of misfortune seem to be hovering over Fisher & Sons, with no sign of any break in the weather!

EPISODE 25
I'LL TAKE YOU

Directed by: Michael Engler
Written by: Jill Soloway

GUEST CAST
Lili Taylor as Lisa
Jeremy Sisto as Billy
Joanna Cassidy as Margaret
Robert Foxworth as Bernard
Glenn Fitzgerald as Aaron Buchbinder
Richard Jenkins as Nathaniel
Ed O'Ross as Nikolai
Justina Machado as Vanessa
Aysia Polk as Taylor
David Norona as Gary Deitman
Eric Bruskotter as Keith's Partner

Efrain Figueroa as Andrew Perez
Gina Morelli as Leticia Perez
Vincent Castellanos as Beauty Parlour Owner
Jennie Vaughn as Abused Wife
Karl Makinen as Abusive Husband
Travis Wester as Henry
Diana Castle as Trust Lawyer
Jim Abele as Social Worker (Mr Sherman)
Austin Nichols as Kyle

Richard Lynch as Commitment Ceremony Presider
Michael E. Dempsey as Sgt Potts
Michael Komurov as Russian Man in Line
Uncredited as Rico's Mom

WHO'S THE STIFF?

Leticia Perfecta Perez, 1922-2002: Expired whilst her perm was setting, underneath a hairdryer in a beauty salon.

PLOT SUMMARY

Nate reads through Brenda's novel, little knowing that it's almost 100 per cent autobiographical. He suggests to Brenda that the novel is a way of getting back at him for Lisa, but Brenda tells him that she started it well before she found out about Lisa.

Keith and David tell Taylor to be on her best behaviour the next day because they are expecting a social worker to visit and assess their suitability as short-term carers for her. Keith later gets some good news from his sergeant – there will be no charges against him for the shooting a few months ago. Claire tells Ruth that she's going to go on a tour of the art school, and Ruth says she wants to go on record as supporting her if she decides to go. Claire's tour is taken by a student called Henry, who advises her to really make the effort in her application, including getting some references, as the school is so popular. The only alumnus from the college that she knows is Billy Chenowith. Claire realises that the art school is really for her when she spots another repainted hearse in the student parking lot!

Ruth makes plans for how much time she and Nikolai will be spending together, but her continual attention seems to be all too much for him to cope with.

Nate visits Aaron Buchbinder to discuss his funeral details. Aaron opts for cremation as it sounds the easiest and cleanest method. When Nate asks if there will be many people at the ceremony, Aaron bitterly tells him that he's always found it difficult to make connections with people. Nate tells Aaron that he will visit him every day until he dies.

Leticia Perez's son Andrew comes to Fisher & Sons to make the final arrangements for his mother. Her pre-need arrangement asks for a specific type of casket, one that looks a bit 'downmarket', but Andrew tries to pay for a more expensive casket so that he isn't embarrassed by the funeral. Both David and Rico (who grew up living near to Mrs Perez) stand firm and say that they legally cannot change Mrs Perez's final wishes. As Andrew Perez leaves, angry at them for not letting him spend money, Rico remembers the first time he met Nathaniel, when he came to Fisher & Sons with his mother to arrange his father Mauricio's funeral back in 1992. His father suffered a major facial and head injury, but the reconstruction work made him look perfect again – at that moment, Rico knew what his calling was.

Worrying about the visit by the social worker, Keith tries to 'de-gay' his apartment, removing videotapes of 'The Wiz' and the paintings of semi-nude men from the walls. The social worker is quite curt and brusque with them until he asks where they got their coffee table from as he leaves. Even Taylor picks up on the fact that 'that man was totally gay!'

Claire visits Gary Deitman and tells him that she's made the application to art school and that she's really excited about it. However, she's shocked to find out that Gary has been let go by the school district – cutbacks mean that he no longer has a job.

Margaret invites Brenda over to talk through the vows she's writing for her re-commitment ceremony with Bernard. Margaret asks Brenda if she has 'the magnet' feeling towards Nate – when Brenda fails to make eye contact with her mother, Margaret tells her to get out of the relationship if that feeling isn't there. Later, all of their family and friends assemble for the ceremony. Despite the new-age language, it's actually heart-warming, and only Brenda remains steadfastly cynical about the whole thing (even Billy thinks it's 'sweet'). Bernard and Nate have a heart-to-heart about what makes relationships work. Bernard still can't believe his luck that Margaret forgave him for his stupid mid-life crisis.

Rico and Vanessa are very pleasantly shocked to discover that Mrs Perez has left them $149,000 in her will. Neither of them had the faintest idea she thought that highly of them.

When Ruth and Nikolai go to the cinema, they end up choosing to go to separate films – Ruth to *Murder by Numbers* and Nikolai to *Blade II*. It seems that they are growing further and further apart. After a short while in her own cinema, Ruth comes to her senses and walks into Nikolai's cinema. She tells him she knows he doesn't really love her, and breaks up with him. To cover up her tears, she goes back into her cinema to watch the end of her weepie film.

Billy comes over to see Claire with his letter of recommendation for her application to art school. Billy admits that he has feelings for her, but tells her that he wants to make sure that he knows her for as long as possible, and that he's scared of using his 'super power of fucking things up'. He tells her that he reckons she has no idea how beautiful she really is.

On a call to a domestic abuse case, Keith loses his temper and beats the abusive husband up.

It's the viewing for Mrs Perez. Andrew Perez is at first dismissive and angry at Rico – his mother left all of her inheritance to a stranger.

Claire takes a framed photograph of herself – one that Billy said was especially beautiful – and places it outside Gary Deitman's office as a leaving present for him.

Kyle, one of the skateboard guys who slept with Brenda, sees her and Nate chatting on her veranda and comes over to see if he can get some more pot. As Kyle leaves, Nate notices the yin and yang symbol on his baseball cap, and makes the connection with the 'fiction' that Brenda has been writing. All of a sudden, the pain and horror and angst of her behaviour and the negativity of their relationship comes spilling out in an argument of epic proportions, accusations and recrimination: 'I'm sick to death of you using it [Brenda's messed-up childhood] as an excuse for you to act like a fucking cunt from hell!' Nate rises to Brenda's bait and throws his engagement ring at her in a moment of pure 'cliché' before walking out.

Nate goes to see Aaron, but the young man is on the verge of death. Nate's mobile rings: David has just heard that Kroehner has gone bankrupt. He's delighted that the good guys seem to finally have won. Keith meanwhile is questioned – on formal videotape –about his actions towards the abusive husband earlier that day.

Back at home, Ruth is cleaning maniacally when Lisa calls. Lisa tells Ruth that she's become a grandmother to a baby girl called Maia. Ruth immediately goes over to visit, for once seeing the joy of a new life reflecting back into her own.

THE PRODIGAL SON

Oh dear. As all the lies and horror that have been building up over the past few months come pouring out, Nate does the only thing that he possibly can do, and walks out on Brenda. As Ruth learned during her first meeting of The Plan, in order to rebuild a house, it's sometimes necessary to knock it down to its very foundations and rebuild from there. The argument between Nate and Brenda doesn't just demolish their relationship, it drops a nuclear bomb on it.

MOMMY, DEAREST

Ruth finally realises that something has to be done about her relationship with Nikolai. Doing a typical 'Ruth' thing, she takes control and terminates the relationship herself. Thankfully, Ruth soon has another avenue to direct her energies in – she has another baby to look after, her granddaughter Maia.

TEENAGE KICKS

Claire's realisation that she might actually make a career as an artist is a wonderful character development. Instead of panicking about Billy's declaration of love for her, she even handles *that* news well too. Understanding that she finally has some kind of control over her own destiny, Claire symbolically cuts the ties to her past by leaving a photo of herself for Gary Deitman. It's time to give up childish things and blossom as a young woman…

DREAM ON, DREAMER

Rico has a flashback to the intake meeting at Fisher & Sons when his father died.

SOUNDTRACK

Shakira – 'Suerte' (Leticia passes away under the hairdryer)

TelepopMusik – 'Breathe' (Nate reads some of Brenda's book)

Lena Horne – 'Back In My Baby's Arms' (David and Keith prepare for the social worker's visit)

Verdi – 'Un Altra Notte' from *Il Trovatore* (Margaret talks to Brenda about the upcoming ceremony)

The Soundtrack Of Our Lives – 'Sister Surround' (Claire takes some self-portraits)

Bill Wells Octet vs. Future Pilot AKA – 'Om Navah Shivaya' (The commitment ceremony)

FirstCom Music Library – 'Super Smooth' (The social worker's visit)

Ali Farka Toure – 'Jangali Famata' (Billy and Brenda's views on their parents)

Ali Farka Toure – 'ASCO' (Nate and Bernard toast new beginnings)

Mariachi All Stars – 'Flor Silvestre' (Andrew is angry when he discovers Rico's inheritance)

Street Walkin' Cheetahs – 'Automatic' (Keith assaults a suspected wife-beater)

Mariachi All Stars – 'El Preso' (Rico puts photos of his kids in Leticia's coffin)

ISN'T THAT WHATSHISNAME?

You can see **Vincent Castellanos** (Beauty Parlour Owner) getting eaten by a giant snake (possibly!) in *Anaconda* (Luis Llosa, 1997).

UNANSWERED QUESTIONS

✝ Is this the end for Nate and Brenda?
✝ Is this the end for Ruth and Nikolai?
✝ Is this the beginning of something between Claire and Billy?
✝ Will the social worker recommend that David and Keith be allowed to look after Taylor?
✝ Will Keith's sudden outburst of violence put that decision in jeopardy?

EULOGY

There's a great deal of good news for lots of the characters in this episode – Rico and Vanessa's inheritance, the collapse of Kroehner, and Claire's realisation about what she may want to do with the rest of her life. However, none of these things can distract from the shattering gloom and anguish of the other storylines. This episode is bleak, depressing and utterly, utterly riveting. Rachel Griffiths and Peter Krause have never been more convincing than during their epic argument, as they really get their teeth stuck into some blistering dialogue. In short, this episode is the emotional turning point of the entire second season of *Six Feet Under* – what's still to come will just add to the trauma of these devastating confrontations.

EPISODE 26
THE LAST TIME

Directed by: Alan Ball
Written by: Kate Robin

GUEST CAST
Lili Taylor as Lisa
Glenn Fitzgerald as Aaron Buchbinder
Ed O'Ross as Nikolai
Justina Machado as Vanessa
Grant Show as Scott Axelrod
Marina Black as Parker

Larry Drake as Inspector Gerson
Geoffrey Nauffts as Dr Di Paulo
Deirdre O'Connell as LAC Arts Interviewer
J.P. Pitoc as Crematory Guy
Daniel Roebuck as Male Sex Addict
Patrice Walters as Anaesthesiologist
Allison Jean Kyler as Claire's Dance Double

WHO'S THE STIFF?

Aaron Buchbinder, 1976-2002: After a long and painful struggle
with pancreatic cancer, Aaron dies in his hospital bed whilst Nate
holds him, repeatedly saying, 'It's OK.'

PLOT SUMMARY

Nate lies alone in his bed, still trying to come to terms with splitting up with Brenda and being a new father. As the family have breakfast, they are shocked to discover that he hasn't even seen his daughter yet. Angry at the way he has been pushed away, Nate goes for a drive on his motorbike and sees Aaron, who dies in his arms.

The shock of watching Aaron die makes Nate book an appointment with his doctor to take some treatment for his AVM. At the same time, an investigator arrives to do a spot check on Fisher & Sons. He discovers Rico and Vanessa eating in the embalming room. He also discovers that Aaron Buchbinder's body has been left unrefrigerated – owing to the fridge being full. It's clear that the spot check has landed them in lots of trouble. The inspector gives Fisher & Sons two weeks to replace their drainage system or the business will be forced to shut down.

Claire waits for her interview for art school. She rambles a bit at her interview, and bursts into tears when she explains that expressing herself through art is her way of dealing with her father's death and the stress of Gabe's behaviour.

Nate takes Aaron's body to the crematorium, but he's unable to 'press the button' today as the furnace is out of action. The guy tells him to come back the following day. David is shocked when he returns home to discover that not only was Keith suspended from work, but Taylor has gone to live with Keith's parents.

Brenda goes to a sex addicts' support group. Whilst there, she's amazed to see Scott Axelrod, the guy who gave Brenda his business card some months back. She reintroduces herself to him as 'Candice', but he can't remember her at all, informing her that he had sex with over 200 women last year. Over a meal at Brenda's, Scott is glad to discover they didn't have sex. Brenda tells him that she doesn't feel that she's 'sick' (as the sex addict course tells her). She confesses that she doesn't want to be one of those 'horrible people who walk around in pain all the time'.

The cheapest quote that Nate finds to replace their drainage system is over $30,000. Unable to see any way to pay it within the two-week timescale, Nate and David tell Rico that they will have to shut down temporarily and advise him to try and find some other short-term work. Hopefully they will be able to re-employ him when they reopen, provided he is still free to come back to them.

Nate's doctor gives him some bad news – his AVM has bled into a critical part of his brain. Instead of an embolisation, he now recommends immediate surgery to stop the bleed from killing him. He books Nate in for surgery two days later. That afternoon, Nate goes back to the crematorium to press the button for Aaron. Realising that the surgery may actually kill him, Nate returns home to collect Ruth so that he can visit his daughter (Ruth having a set of keys for Lisa's house). Lisa is delighted that Nate has finally taken an interest in Maia. Ruth takes a photo of her son and granddaughter together. Nate apologises to Lisa for Ruth's over-interest in Maia, but Lisa says Ruth has been a godsend – so loving and funny.

On the journey back from Lisa's, Nate tells Ruth about his condition and the surgery he's going to have to go through. She's upset that he never told her about the AVM. Ruth tells Claire that David will go to her graduation ceremony with a video camera to record it, whilst she goes to be with Nate at the hospital. Planning all eventualities, Nate gets David to help him fill out his pre-need agreement. Nate tells David he wants Rabbi Ari to conduct his service rather than Father Jack. They are both really scared about what may happen. David goes home to Keith's, but there's no comfort for him there – Keith is uncommunicative and doesn't want to speak.

Ruth quits her job at Nikolai's, telling him that she wants to spend time with Maia. Nikolai says that's good for him too, and offers to pay back a bit of the money he owes her every week.

Nate tells Claire how impressed he is with her photography. They have a heart-to-heart about relationships and Claire says that he can carry on giving her advice but he shouldn't try to laud his experience over her.

Rico buys into Fisher & Sons – $75,000 for a 25 per cent share in the company – after Nate reminds David that he may very soon need an extra partner.

Brenda and Nate finally have a conversation where they both acknowledge that a lot of what each other said during their argument was true. Brenda tells him that she's been going to sex addiction classes, and Nate confirms that he really was using their relationship in a co-dependent way. Brenda says she really loves him and that she probably wouldn't have slept around if she didn't. She was scared of feeling something 'real'. Nate tells her that he really loves her and that being with her makes him feel 'more' than he does with other people – more love, more fear. He then tells Brenda about his surgery, lying that it's just a routine embolisation rather than emergency surgery to save his life. He says she can't come to the hospital to be with him.

Keith and David argue violently about their relationship and whose fault it is for them no longer being close. Their argument turns into spontaneous passionate sex.

Claire is delighted when Parker tells her that she's been turned down for Yale because her 'stand-in' admitted sitting exams for payment. It looks as though her best friend won't be leaving LA after all!

Ruth and Nate cry together before heading off to the hospital, whilst David and Claire smoke some dope before going to her graduation. They think about what's happening to Nate, and decide to skip the ceremony, heading straight to the hospital instead. Ruth, David and Claire wait together at the hospital for news. Simultaneously, Brenda clears out her house, packing all of her belongings into a small red car, and drives away.

A shaven-headed Nate lies on the operating table as he gets his anaesthetic for surgery. His world goes white.

Nate is jogging along an empty highway. A bus – *the* bus – pulls up alongside him. Nate strolls towards the doors of the bus. The door opens, and Nate stands there, deciding whether or not to get on board.

DREAM ON, DREAMER

Is Nate's final dream of the bus really just a dream, or something far more... terminal?

SOUNDTRACK

Bottlefly – 'Got 2 B Luv' (Nate's clock radio wakes him up)
Irene Cara – 'Flashdance... What A Feeling' (Claire's *Flashdance* fantasy)

Bob Mould – 'Sound On Sound' (Claire listens to music as she waits for her interview)

Soul Hooligan – 'Algebra' (Nate delivers Aaron's body to the crematorium)

Strike Boys – 'Go Back Home' (Brenda has lunch with Scott Axelrod)

Grant Lee Phillips – 'Humankind' (Nate and Claire's heart-to-heart)

Timo Maas – 'To Get Down (Fatboy Slim Remix)' (Claire and Parker discuss plans for the future)

Flaming Lips – 'Fight Test' (David videos Claire)

Ian Brown – 'Neptune' (Claire and David decide to go to the hospital)

SEX, DRUGS AND ROCK 'N' ROLL

David and Claire share a joint to ease their fear about Nate's surgery. David and Keith's violent argument turns into a violent coupling – just how healthy can their relationship possibly be?

THE BRIGHT SIDE OF DEATH

Nate: This must be the final mind-fuck of Mitzi Dalton Huntley…

ISN'T THAT WHATSHISNAME?

Larry Drake (Inspector Gerson) played Benny Stulwicz in *L.A. Law*.

UNANSWERED QUESTIONS

✠ Where is Brenda going?
✠ Will Nate get on the bus?

EULOGY

So that's it – the end of the second series of the most consistently high-quality programme ever made on television. But what are we to make of it? At the time of writing, the third series of *Six Feet Under* is yet to go into production, so there are no 'spoilers' about what may happen to the Fishers and their partners and friends. Despite that, here's my suggestions as to what *might* occur:

- ✝ Nate won't 'get on the bus', but the impact of the emergency surgery will be long-lasting
- ✝ David and Keith's relationship will be tested much further – unless there are some major changes, they won't survive
- ✝ Ruth won't go back to working with Nikolai, and there's not much chance that their relationship will be revived
- ✝ Brenda will come back, but it will take a lot of hard work on both her and Nate's parts before there's any chance of a reconciliation
- ✝ The presence of Lisa may put Nate into a romantic triangle
- ✝ Claire's new life at college will be complicated by her feelings for Billy
- ✝ Rico's new position as a partner at Fisher & Sons will bring him into major conflict with Nate and (especially) David

The wonderful thing about *Six Feet Under* is that my guesses are almost certainly going to be proved wide of the mark. The talented production team have made sure that the plotlines and characters have continued to surprise and entertain us for the first two seasons. Here's to Season Three, and many more.

APPENDIX

AWARDS AND NOMINATIONS

Since *Six Feet Under* first appeared on television, it has consistently been nominated for almost every award going. This is a *partial* list (at time of writing, September 2002) of the awards that *Six Feet Under* has so far won, and the ones it has been nominated for. Many of these awards have yet to be announced, so I hope the *Six Feet Under* offices have got lots of room on their mantelpiece...

American Film Institute
AFI Actor of the Year (Male) – Michael C. Hall   *Nominated*
AFI TV Drama Series of the Year   *Nominated*

American Latino Media Arts Awards
Outstanding Actor in a TV Series – Freddy Rodriguez   *Nominated*
Outstanding TV Drama Series   *Nominated*

Cinema Audio Society
Outstanding Sound Mixing for Television   *Winner*

Costume Designers Guild
Excellence for TV Costume Design (Contemporary)   *Nominated*

Directors' Guild of America
DGA Award   *Winner*

Emmy Awards

Outstanding Lead Actor in TV Drama	
– Peter Krause	*Nominated*
Outstanding Lead Actor in TV Drama	
– Michael C. Hall	*Nominated*
Outstanding Lead Actress in TV Drama	
– Rachel Griffiths	*Nominated*
Outstanding Lead Actress in TV Drama	
– Frances Conroy	*Nominated*
Outstanding Supporting Actor in TV Drama	
– Freddy Rodriguez	*Nominated*
Outstanding Supporting Actress in TV Drama	
– Lauren Ambrose	*Nominated*
Outstanding Guest Actress in TV Drama	
– Patricia Clarkson	*Won*
Outstanding Guest Actress in TV Drama	
– Illeana Douglas	*Nominated*
Outstanding Guest Actress in TV Drama	
– Lili Taylor	*Nominated*
Outstanding Drama Series	*Nominated*
Outstanding Direction – Alan Ball (pilot episode)	*Won*
Outstanding Art Direction	*Nominated*
Outstanding Casting for a Drama Series	*Nominated*

Gay & Lesbian Alliance Against Defamation

GLAAD Media Award	*Won*

Golden Globes

Best Supporting Actress – Rachel Griffiths	*Won*
Best Television Drama Series	*Won*
Best Lead Actor – Peter Krause	*Nominated*

Golden Satellite Awards

Best Television Drama Series	*Nominated*

Screen Actors Guild Awards
Outstanding Performance by Lead Actor
    – Peter Krause   *Nominated*
Outstanding Performance by Ensemble Cast   *Nominated*